Financial Freedom Investing

You Want to Invest but Have No Idea Where to Start? Understand Investment Tools, Avoid the Most Common Mistakes and Reach Financial Freedom (No Savings Needed!)

© Copyright 2019 – All rights reserved

The following eBook is reproduced below with the goal of providing information that is as accurate and reliable as possible. Regardless, purchasing this eBook can be seen as consent to the fact that both the publisher and the author of this book are in no way experts on the topics discussed within and that any recommendations or suggestions that are made herein are for entertainment purposes only. Professionals should be consulted as needed prior to undertaking any of the action endorsed herein.

This declaration is deemed fair and valid by both the American Bar Association and the Committee of Publishers Association and is legally binding throughout the United States.

Furthermore, the transmission, duplication, or reproduction of any of the following work including specific information will be considered an illegal act irrespective of if it is done electronically or in print. This extends to creating a secondary or tertiary copy of the work or a recorded copy and is only allowed with express written consent from the Publisher. All additional right reserved.

The information in the following pages is broadly considered to be a truthful and accurate account of facts and as such any inattention, use or misuse of the information in question by the reader will render any resulting actions solely under this purview. There are no scenarios in which the publisher or the original author of this work can be in any fashion deemed liable for any hardship or damages that may befall them after undertaking information described herein

Additionally, the information in the following pages is intended only for informational purposes and should thus be thought of as universal. As befitting its nature, it is presented without assurance regarding its prolonged validity or interim quality. Trademarks that are mentioned are done without written consent and can in no way be considered an endorsement from the trademark holder.

Table of Contents

Introduction 5

Chapter 1: The Building Blocks of Financial Freedom 9
   Important Mindset Shifts to Start Accruing Wealth 9
   Essential Steps for Achieving Financial Freedom 11
   How to Set Your Financial Goals 14
   Setting Your Short-Term and Long-Term Goals 18
   10 Ways to Get Out of Debt ASAP 19

Chapter 2: How to Budget the Right Way 24
   How to Find a Budget That Works for You 24
   6 Must-Know Budgeting Methods to Never Lose Track of Money Again 26
   Which Budget Is Right for You? 30
   7 Ways to Make Budgeting More Enjoyable 31
   7 Important Steps for Building Good Credit 35

Chapter 3: Investing 101 39
   Types of Investments to Add to Your Portfolio 39
   Tips on Choosing the Right Stocks for You 47
   What Is an Investment Plan? 50
   The 5 Best Stock Trading Strategies of All Time 51
   8 Worst Investing Mistakes to Avoid 52

Chapter 4: Dividend Stocks 56
   When a Company Pays Dividends 56
   Different Types of Dividends 57
   Choosing Stocks That Pay High Dividends 60
   How to Find the Best Dividend Stocks for Your Portfolio 62

Do Not Make These 10 Dividend Investing Mistakes.................... 63
What You Need to Know About Dividend Tax Rates..................... 66
Ordinary vs. Qualified Dividends.. 67

Chapter 5: Day Trading 69
What Is Day Trading? 69
How to Start Day Trading 70
Day Trading Strategies.. 74

Chapter 6: Real Estate Investing 80
Increasing Your Property Value 80
Making Money From Rental Property 81
How to Select a Target Market... 87
10 Important Features of Profitable Real Estate 92
Top 15 Real Estate Investing Strategies.. 95

Chapter 7: Other Ways to Grow Wealth 98
How to Start Investing in Exchange-Traded Funds (ETFs).......... 98
Start Making Money Now with Peer-to-Peer Lending................ 101
The 10 Best Strategies for Trading Cryptocurrencies............... 103
7 Must-Have Apps for Modern-Day Investors 107

Conclusion 110

Introduction

All of us seek financial freedom for different reasons. It could be that you want this freedom so that you can secure enough money to live comfortably in your retirement years. Others may be looking to purchase a new home, and still others may be planning a nest egg for their later years.

Planning how you will support yourself in your retirement can be stressful, and most people have money concerns looming over their heads. How many times have you turned on the news only to hear that some wealthy individual has just filed for bankruptcy? You might be wondering, *If he can't manage it with all his money, then what chance do I have?*

It is a legitimate concern. A look back through our recent history tells us that times have changed. We can no longer rely on job security to carry us through our lives. Jobs that you could stay on for 30 years or more and retire on a handsome pension plan are now few and far between. If we want financial freedom in this modern world, we need to learn how to think differently.

The challenge that we all face is how to get that financial security without relying on the traditional methods past generations took for granted. Those days are over, and we all need to plan our financial future more creatively.

In such situations, it can be difficult to know where to start. Maybe you're thinking about investing, but you don't know enough about it to make wise decisions. You're afraid of losing your hard-earned money on a high-risk gamble. Or maybe you're just tired of living paycheck to paycheck and you see that you need to think differently.

Or you're getting older and your body doesn't want to work as hard as it has before. Whether you're getting up in years and planning for retirement or you're just starting out and you're saving for a big purchase or investment, it makes sense that you start here with us.

There are many ways that we can meet this challenge. We have all learned how difficult it is to just put your money in a savings account and wait for it to grow. The interest rates they offer is such a pittance that you probably feel like you're actually paying the bank to hold your money rather than making anything off of it.

If you've thought about any of these things before, then you've come to the right place. You will be joining many others of like minds who have the same questions. In the following pages, we will show you how you can achieve a level of financial wealth that will put you on a sure footing, where you won't have to worry about your finances. Here, you will find:

- A beginner-friendly guide to investing and various investment options
- Ideas for how to make more money without much extra work needed
- Tips on making both short- and long-term goals and why they are important
- Essential information that can apply to a wide variety of financial needs.

There are plenty of alternatives to growing your cash and setting up a secure future for yourself. The answers are out there for anyone who has the wherewithal to look. They are not new, magical, or even mystical. This book is designed specifically to teach you some of those alternatives and how utilizing them can make a huge difference in helping you to achieve your financial freedom.

We've been taught that the fastest way to any destination is in a straight line. Unlike savings, however, this is not always the case. Investing requires that you take a few turns here or there and you may very well hit a few bumps in the road along the way. But, if you stay the course, your investment decisions could easily help you achieve financial freedom much sooner than you might think.

Once you apply the principles in this book, the rewards for your hard work will definitely be worth it. You will have:

- Freedom from money worries
- Freedom from debt
- Freedom to do what you want
- Freedom from painful anxiety
- A better relationship with money
- Freedom to live a life based on your values
- More confidence in your ability to manage money
- Less stress, which means better health
- Freedom to grow wealthy on your own terms

If you're ready to change your life for the better — to stop merely existing in this world rather than truly living — then it is time for you to take the next step. The sooner you start, the sooner you will see yourself journeying that road to financial freedom. It is my responsibility to guide you step by step to that dream lifestyle you want.

So, if you're ready to change your life, and move onto something that's even better, then it's time to download this book today. It's totally up to you to take back control of your life and actually win the rat race for a change. So, what are you waiting for? Now is the time to change your life for the better by letting us help you to gain financial freedom.

Chapter 1: The Building Blocks of Financial Freedom

Most goals should have a specific end date, but things aren't so simple when it comes to money. For one thing, your ultimate goal of financial freedom needs to be broken down into a lot of smaller goals. Not only that, you will have to live life in a very specific way in order to maintain those circumstances after you have acquired it.

Overwhelmed? Don't be, as it all starts simply by having a specific mindset.

Important Mindset Shifts to Start Accruing Wealth

There is nothing unique about finances. While it may be elusive to some people, it is really just a matter of mastering the fundamentals. Whether you're Jeff Bezos or you're the cleaning lady, the rules of the game are exactly the same: mastering the fundamentals and consistently applying them.

This is not just about saving up for a new car or for a fabulous vacation one day. Yes, savings is very important in the grand scheme of things, but saving just for the sake of saving is not always your best option. Your first goal is to make the most of your money, not just for today or the next few years, but for the remainder of your life. This requires a huge shift in perspective. You're in it for the long haul and that means that what you need for today may not be what is needed in 10 years or 20 or 50.

Have you ever heard of people who seem to have struck it rich overnight? Chances are you have. You might even have personally known a few of them. Some of them may have been positioned in high paying jobs where they could sock away a lot of cash whenever they wanted, but others may have started with little or nothing. They may have been the local garbage collector, the housekeeper, or a waitress at a nearby diner.

Aside from those who have acquired their wealth by winning the lottery, others have managed to achieve their money seemingly without effort. However, if you look closely, their imagined overnight success came after years of careful planning. There is nothing more important to your success than changing your mental mindset. You will have to switch from the common ideas that are the norm in today's society to something that will guarantee that you get improved results.

Essential Steps for Achieving Financial Freedom

1. **Make a detailed plan**

   One of the first steps you must do is to create a plan. Your success should not be something you get by accident or by surprise. Each step of your path should be made and achieved by design. Rather than allowing things to just happen, start thinking about everything you do and any possible consequences that can occur.

   Imagine designing your dream home. You've probably thought about it for years. You know every detail, down to the shape and design of each knob and fixture. If it's truly your dream house, you've already thought about what it will take to repair it when things go wrong, what colors to paint it and how often. You know which rooms to give your kids and every feature you'll have in your kitchen.

   You have to take the same extra care when planning for your financial future. You're not thinking just for today but are planning for the future. How many years will it take for you to reach your goal and the kind of effort you will need to maintain it? With a detailed plan, you'll know what to do today, tomorrow, next month, next year, and each year after that. You'll keep doing this until you reach a point where your money will start to work for you.

2. **Get out of the paycheck-to-paycheck mindset**

   We've been programmed from childhood to think in terms of survival. Perhaps it's human nature, but many of us who are struggling to survive tend to focus on the negatives. Even though events may not have automatically come to mind, it's easy to fall into the sky is falling approach to everything. The problem with this line of thinking is that it limits us. When you are concerned, your mind focuses on holding onto every penny you have, investment opportunities can easily pass you by because you're only thinking in the moment.

Wealthy people do not think this way. Because they have a plan, their minds are focused on the next step, which will automatically lead them to prosperity. Their minds are free to explore other possibilities, and they see opportunities all around them. They examine each one and process every aspect of it until they reach a breakthrough where they can see how to use it to grow what they have rather than holding onto everything they have earned.

3. **Don't always play it safe**

In line with the survival line of thinking is the need to seek security. Yes, money can bring you a level of security. You know that if you have enough money, you have a roof over your head, food in your stomach and clothes on your back. However, if your mind never looks beyond your safety net, you may miss many profitable opportunities. No one ever achieved financial independence while sitting on the fence. Playing it safe cuts you off from many avenues you can take to wealth.

This doesn't mean that you should throw caution to the wind. You still need to think things through and analyze every opportunity to make sure that it's a risk that will pay off in the end. Being a risk-taker doesn't mean being foolhardy. It means that you're going to have to step out on faith and believe in your decisions even when you don't know the outcome.

Courage has been defined as the willingness to take action when you cannot control the outcome. Take the time to read a few background stories of successful people that you admire, and you'll find the same pattern. They recognized an opportunity and took action, often before anyone else saw the potential. By the time others joined in, they were already well on their way to amassing great wealth.

4. **Stop thinking about spending and start thinking about saving**

This is a mindset that's quite ingrained. If your parents taught you well, then chances are you didn't spend every penny of your allowance when you were a kid. You might have had to save up for that new bike or computer game. Sadly, many young people grow up spending every last penny they have for the things they want. In most cases, the things they want don't last for very long. So, when those things are gone, so is their money.

The average American household spends 110% of their income. When they overspend, they usually find themselves deep in debt with credit cards and loans from friends and family members. If you have a spendthrift attitude, your attempts to acquire wealth will inevitably dig a hole for yourself that will be almost impossible to get out of.

There have been numerous studies that show that you need to save between 20–30% of your income to reach the point where your money will actually work for you. Taking 20% of your income and setting it aside and then living off the rest is not that hard. Once you make this adjustment, you're not likely to even notice the difference.

5. Stop hoping and start doing

Hope is a powerful motivator, but there will always comes a time when you need to take action. You need to stop thinking about what you want to do and become proactive. Even the smallest step in the right direction can be rewarding.

Most people do not realize that they are paralyzed by hope. They spend their time talking and sharing their ideas, but they rarely get beyond that point. Rather than spending your energy sharing your plans with others, start gathering what you need to execute your plan.

Just like everything else in life, nothing we say or do happens without it first being a thought. If you've developed bad financial habits in the past, they were started with your thinking. So, in order to gain financial freedom, it is necessary for you to change the way you think about money. By changing your thoughts, you can accomplish great things in an amazingly short amount of time. You'll start off slowly at first, but gradually your plans will pick up momentum and as the time passes you see small successes along your path, you'll start to feel more confident and you'll see your freedom just beyond that light at the end of the tunnel.

How to Set Your Financial Goals

Most people do not fully understand money or how it works. They think that having cash on hand is security and cannot grasp how saving it may not be the best choice for them. Anything you do to increase your financial security has to have a goal. If you are saving money, you need to have a goal for that. Money is not the end-all of anything you do. It is the means to an end. If money is never used for any purpose, you end up either wasting it on frivolous things or hoarding it. In the end, you may leave this earth and all your money behind for someone else to use.

Take a long hard look at your goals and try to determine where your money should be going. Actually, sitting down and putting pen to paper can be a little scary, but it brings you face to face with your financial realities.

When you're laying out what you plan to do with your money and setting your goals, it can be kind of cathartic. But before you do anything, make sure your boots are firmly planted on the ground. Without clearly defined goals, you may end up jumping ship and splurging the first chance you get. It could be very easy to end up watching that wealth as it slips away, buried under a mountain of debt. So, when setting your goals, start with a realistic but flexible plan. What you might want today may not be what you want later in life, make sure you have some wiggle room to work with.

- **Determine how much money you have to start with.** It doesn't matter if your goals are short or long-term, you need to know your starting point. Be realistic about how much you have to work with. If you don't, it is quite likely you'll work your way to the bottom of your wallet before you reach your final destination. Remember, your goal is to stop living from paycheck to paycheck, so you don't want to start blind.

  Take some time to sit down and get a realistic look at your current financial situation. Your starting point should consist of 1) how much money you have on hand and in your bank accounts, IRAs, or investments; include physical assets that you may have already paid off. 2) List all of the debts you still have outstanding. Consider credit card balances, mortgages, student loans, child support or any other financial obligations that you have to meet.

Take the total amount you owe and deduct it from your total assets to get your net worth. This is your starting point. Don't worry if this number is in the negative, the goal of reading this book is to change that.

- **Create a budget.** Now that you know what you're worth financially, you have a starting point and you can figure out a budget. Your budget will be a detailed outline of all the expenses that you have and how much you will pay towards them every month.

- **Make sure you cover everything.** That includes that $10.00/month video streaming service that you take for granted. In addition to obvious expenses, include utilities, insurance policies, food, gas, and entertainment. Don't leave anything out. If you're not sure of what to include on the list, go back over the last few months of receipts and take a look. This list will be the foundation of your budget.

  Take a look at your starting figure. If you don't like it, then go back through your list to see if you can cut some of those expenses. What can you eliminate? Cable? Streaming? Subscription accounts? You might even be able to forego eating out and opt to do more cooking at home.

  This doesn't mean that you have to give up on your good times, you just have to be willing to sacrifice a little to get better returns. Once you've decided what you can do without, you'll see that final number getting larger. You now have a budget!

  Now that you know how much you have to work with, you can start setting realistic goals.

- **Set practical goals.** Financial goals are not the same for everyone, so no one can tell you what to shoot for. However, there are some practical goals you might want to consider. You can always add to them later if you want. The most common goals you'll find people set are:

    o   Establishing an emergency fund
    o   Getting out of debt
    o   Planning for retirement
    o   Buying a home or a car
    o   Taking a dream vacation

You can choose for yourself which ones should be addressed first, but as long as the first three are addressed you should be able to find the security you're looking for. Follow these basic suggestions to help you get started.

Goal 1: Establishing an emergency fund. If you've done your budget well, you'll at least have a few dollars to dedicate to an emergency fund. In the beginning, it may not be much. Maybe $5 or $10 each paycheck. However, if you are consistent, you'll be amazed at just how much you can accumulate with a steady deposit of a few bucks into your account.

You decide just how much money you want to have in your emergency fund. No one can tell you how much you need, but a general guideline is three to six months' worth of living expenses should be set aside. If you have good job security that may be enough, but if you're on a precarious footing with your job, then you might decide on a little more.

Goal 2: Pay Down Your Debt. It is easy to get bogged down in bills every month and it can be very discouraging to watch your account bleed out every payday. Some people see money as electricity, and they are merely the wire it passes through. It goes out as fast, if not faster, than its coming in.

The best way to solve this problem is to take aim on those bills and pay them off. Being-debt free may feel like an impossible task, but if you're willing to make a few sacrifices in the beginning, even a few extra dollars added to each payment will start to see that balance slowly begin to. Just make sure that you don't spend any of your emergency fund money in the interim.

Goal 3: Planning for retirement. You want to think about your future, even if you're a long way from its reality. If you haven't thought much about this yet, then you're not alone. If you love your job and can't imagine life without it, then maybe you can get by, but by and large, the majority of people want to see a day when they do not have to get up and trudge to work all day. They want to spend their later years doing the things they love and making the most out of their lives.

The sooner you start this plan, the easier it will be to get to that final day at work when you can claim your life back. It doesn't matter how old you are, it's never too early to start planning for retirement. If you have a job that offers a nice 401(k) plan all the better. However, even if they don't, you can still set aside money for those later years on your own. Your future self will thank you profusely for it.

Setting Your Short-Term and Long-Term Goals

Now for the fun part. Once you've got the adult things out of the way, it's time to think about supporting the kid in you. This is where you decide how you will use that accumulated wealth to enhance your quality of life. Think about the kinds of things that will give you enjoyment and satisfaction in life.

It doesn't matter what your goals are, it's time to start making a list to help you to categorize them in order of importance. Start by making a list of all the things you want to do, then separate them into different categories:

1. **Short-term**: goals that can be filled within just a few years. Vacations, buying a car, or taking a gourmet cooking class.

2. **Long-term**: goals that may take you 10 years or more to achieve. Buying a house or developing rental property.

By detailing your heart's desire on paper, you put them front and center in your life. Make sure when you write down your goals that you also set an estimated timeline for achieving it. The timeline is what will motivate you to move forward, do the necessary research and take the steps to achieve it without procrastinating.

10 Ways to Get Out of Debt ASAP

The fun part of budgeting and financial planning is in your dreams. But if you're serious about obtaining financial freedom you need to get out of debt first. This can be difficult when you consider that most people today are in debt to the tune of nearly $25,000. That's a lot of bills to pay.

Because people tend to spend more than they earn, the accumulated debt in most cases is the result of credit use to make up the difference. If you want to find the wealth you're looking for, you can no longer hide behind your credit to get the things you need. All it takes is one disaster or unfortunate event and you'll be well on your way to bankruptcy.

1. **Don't just pay the minimum payment.** Take a look at the interest rate on your credit card statement. In most cases, it is 15% or higher. At that rate, if you pay only the minimum payment amount each month, it could take you years to pay it off. This is one of the main reasons why people are unable to see their way clear of credit card bills, but interest rates can be the bane of your existence in other loans too. Think about all the interest you're paying for your student loans, personal loans, or other forms of debt.

    - The best way to pay these bills down faster is to pay more than the minimum payment. You'll not only cut down on the interest you pay, but the additional money you add will help to reduce the principal amount owed speeding up the payment process.

    - Before you completely pay off your debt, check to make sure that your creditor is not going to charge you any prepayment penalties for paying it off early.

2. **Use the snowball method.** If you can find a way to pay more than the minimum monthly payment, you can use the snowball method to pay off your debts. This will not only get the bills paid, but it will boost your sense of accomplishment along the way.

    - List all of your debts from the smallest to the largest. Use all your excess funds to pay off the smallest debt first and make minimum monthly payments on all the other ones. Once the smallest bill is paid off, then take that extra cash and pay it towards the next smallest bill on the list until that one is paid in full.

- In essence, you are snowballing all of your extra money and pushing towards the total amount you owe until you reach a point when you can say you are debt-free.

3. **Get an extra job**. If you can see your way clear to pick up a few extra dollars with an additional job you can actually put a lot more cash in your pocket to pay off those extra bills. It doesn't have to be a regular job where you have to punch a clock every day. Nearly everyone has some specialized skill or talent that they can tap into. Picking up a few weekend jobs a month or freelance assignments can go far in putting extra cash in your pocket.

4. **Downsize your life**. If you're really determined, you can cut your expenses down to the absolute minimum, until all your bills are paid in full. This means you will eliminate all extra spending and just use enough money to get by. If this thought is making your heart race too fast, relax a little. This type of budget is not meant to be a lifetime decision but will only be exercised until you become debt-free.

5. **Have a garage/yard sale**. Everyone has a lot of stuff they no longer have any use for. Take some time and go through your garage, closets, basements, and attics to see what you've got stashed away. You know the saying, "one man's trash is another man's treasure." If you find things in your home that you no longer use and have no realistic expectations of using them in the future, you should have no problem coming up with things to sell.

    a. If you don't have time to set up a yard sale, consider taking your things to a consignment shop or sell them online on sites like eBay, Facebook, or Craigslist.

6. **Negotiate a lower interest rate.** If you're struggling with excessively high interest rates, it may be possible to negotiate for a lower rate. Many people do not think to make such a request, but many credit companies are happy to oblige, especially if you have a good relationship with them.

7. **Transfer your balance.** If you have one credit card with an extremely high bill and you're paying high interest rates on top of that, you may be able to transfer the remaining balance to another card with a lower interest rate. There are even some cards that offer a 0% interest rate for the first 18 months. With that kind of kick, you'll have a lot of extra cash to throw at those bills.

8. **Use unexpected money to pay down debt**. Throughout the year, you may receive additional unexpected income. For example, you might receive an end-of-the-year bonus from your employer, or you may get a nice fat tax refund check. Perhaps a rich uncle has left you a tidy little sum or you get a raise. Whatever the case, it is not money that you have dedicated to your budgetary expenses. Use that money to pay down your debt and you'll be well ahead of the game.

9. **Stop unnecessary spending**. More often than not, the credit card balance doesn't go down because you keep adding to it. Taking the time to examine how you use your credit card can give you a good picture of your spending habits. By looking back over your past expenditures, you can decide for yourself if the debt was really worth it. Maybe you could have settled for a regular cup of coffee rather than a mocha Frappuccino. Brown bagging it to work can keep you from going out to eat saving you tons of money. By eliminating expensive habits, you can cut your overall expenses down to something that is much more manageable.

10. **Avoid temptation**. We all have things that are hard to resist. Still, you can almost guarantee that with all the marketing and advertising going on around you every day, the carrot that society is dangling in front of your eyes every day will tempt you. When you're trying to pay down debt, it is best to try to avoid those temptations wherever you go. If you're drawn into your favorite restaurant on your way home from work every day, try taking a different route. If you see the same tempting commercial on when you watch TV, consider changing the channel or at least getting up and walking out of the room during commercial breaks.

The bottom line is *you have a choice*. You can continue to take the easy road and just stick your head in the sand, pretending you do not see your financial situation, or you can face your debt issues head on. Whether you choose to do it now or are faced to deal with it later, you're going to have to pay your bills. It's better to do it on your own terms.

The main thing to remember is that there is a way out, but don't expect a miracle. With your plans to achieve financial freedom, it's going to take a little hustle on your part, but if you do, you'll be richly rewarded for all your hard work in the end.

Chapter 2: How to Budget the Right Way

Building good credit is essential to your financial future. While it is possible to live in this world without credit, it is not easy. But, getting out of debt and reestablishing your credit is not easy either. It takes careful planning and becoming fully aware off every dollar you spend. The only way to get out of the quagmire is by careful budgeting, but even that can get a little confusing. There are so many different plans for budgeting that it can be overwhelming to know what to do.

The problem is that creating a budget is not as cut and dry as you might believe. Just like not all credit habits are the same, not all approaches to correcting your financial situation will be suitable for you. Yes, the ultimate goal remains consistent: you want to pay down debt, build up a little nest egg, or work towards a major purchase. But reality dictates that there are many roads you can take to get there.

How to Find a Budget That Works for You

Before you can decide on the method that you will apply to your finances, think about the factors that are currently affecting your life. Clearly, a single person living alone will not have as much to worry about as one who has a family to support. You also have to dedicate time to creating a budget and consider the resources you have at your disposal. Below are several budgeting methods you can consider. Read them through and see which one rings true for you. This will help you to determine where you lie on the spectrum so you can plan an effective approach to budgeting going forward.

When you know your starting point, deciding the route to take is much easier. You know what you have to work with and where you want to end up. All that's left is to draw a line on your road map.

1. **Know your values.** Your values consist of what matters to you, the things in your life that you feel you can't live without. Obviously, food, clothing, and shelter would be on the top of this list. Values may differ from person to person. The point is that understanding your values will help you to prioritize what's most important in your budget.

2. **Set your goals.** Your values will give you clear directions on what you should be striving for. Think about what you want your money to do for you in the future, but don't just write down one single long-term goal. Break it up into workable steps. What would you like to accomplish in the next month, three months, six months, a year, three years, five years, 10 years?

3. **Know your income.** How much money do you bring home each pay period – after taxes? This will be the money you will use to determine your spending allowance. You only want to include money that you receive on a regular basis and that you KNOW is coming.

4. **Know your expenses.** Look over your credit card statements, bank records, and store receipts. You can divide your expenses into two categories – fixed and flexible expenses. Fixed expenses would be your rent or mortgage, car payment, credit card bills, and student loans.

   Flexible expenses are a little harder to figure out. These include things like food, clothing, entertainment, etc. The cost varies from one month to the next. You may have to calculate the total amount over several months and then come up with a reasonable average.

> Don't forget about additional expenses that are easily forgotten. These are those costs that you do not pay with regularity; taxes, insurance, subscriptions, etc.

Now, you have all the tools you need to create a workable budget that will help you to meet your needs.

Now comes the part when you have to decide what method will work best for you.

6 Must-Know Budgeting Methods to Never Lose Track of Money Again

As long as the fundamentals of budgeting are covered — tracking expenses, managing income — you have a little leeway in choosing the budgeting method that works for you. If one of them looks like a good fit, then go for it. There's no harm in switching to another one if you find it doesn't quite meet your needs.

1. The Line-Item Budget

> The line-item budget is designed for those who have problems with major spending issues. People who use it are those that seriously need to get out of debt and have no problem with putting all of their expenses into workable categories.
>
> This system requires you to categorize your expenses. You can create as many categories as you need to: household expenses, credit card debt, transportation costs, food, clothing, utilities, grooming, you get the idea. Under each category, list all of the expenses you have to pay.

Create three columns, estimated spending, actual spending, and whatever is left over. When you compare each of these columns, you will be able to measure your progress after each pay period.

Next to each item, assign a dollar amount to be paid monthly. As you make each payment, make a note of it and deduct the amount from the total due. It might be helpful to create an additional bill for incidentals, that way, nothing is left out.

This budgeting method is perfect for the person that has the time and the resources to figure out a lot of details and the dedication to do the extra work that is involved.

2. The 50/30/20 Budget

The 50/30/20 budget has guidelines that aren't as meticulous. However, with the 50/30/20 budget, you dedicate 50% of your income to necessary expenses, 30% to things you want, and 20% to savings.

This method is ideal for those who are not comfortable with a strict budget or they don't have a lot of time to dedicate to doing a line-item budget. Still, it is flexible enough that you know exactly how much you can put away and how much you have to spend on your daily needs. The model should be flexible enough to fit in with your lifestyle.

3. Pay Yourself First

The pay yourself first model takes money from your income and put it into a savings account before you pay for anything else. Even though you pay yourself first, you will still need to know just how much money you need to meet your expenses so that you have enough to cover them.

This method works well for those who find themselves at the end of the month wondering where all of their money has gone. At the same time, it doesn't require you to stick to a strict dollar accounting.

It also works well with those who have an inconsistent monthly income. First, take the average of the last six months of income, then total all of your expenses for the same period, and then subtract the expenses from the income. The remainder is what you can dedicate to your savings.

4. The Envelope System

There is another system that works with a little tighter pull on the purse strings. It works well for those who need a little more discipline to get the job done. The envelope system helps you to cut back on spending too much on non-essentials without having to keep track of every penny you spend. It is a basic cash-based approach to budgeting.

Determine a spending limit for each expense. For example, you could create individual budgets for groceries, clothing, and entertainment. At the start of each month, divide all of your money into these smaller budget categories and place it into labeled envelopes. Anytime you need to purchase something from one of those categories, you pay for it out of that envelope. When the envelope is empty, you have exhausted your budget and there is no more money to make any more purchases until the next payday.

This method works well for those who struggle to control their spending habits or are relying too heavily on credit or debit cards to pay for things. They don't realize how much they are spending until all of their money is gone.

5. Zero-Sum Budget

Then there is the zero-based budget, which is particularly good for anyone who has a tendency to overspend without realizing it. With this plan, you will know exactly how every dollar you spend is being used. In other words, every dollar must have an intended purpose before it leaves your hands, you must account for every penny in order for it to work well.

The system works exactly the way it sounds. On the last day of the month, your budget should always equal zero. So, if at the end of the month, you have money left over, you must stop and find a home for that money.

It works for those people who usually have a little extra cash at the end of the month. Without giving the money a job to do, the tendency to use it for unnecessary things can be a problem. It forces you to stop and think practically about how best to use your funds so that they push you closer to your goals.

6. The No-Budget Budget

This method requires you to be aware of your spending habits. Rather than worrying about how much is being spent in each of your categories, you spend based on your values and what's most important to you.

It works well for those who may already be pretty frugal and somewhat disciplined about the money they spend.

Start by creating an outline for everything that you feel comfortable spending your money on. Anything that is not in line with what you feel is important or essential should not make it on this list.

For example, you might be someone who prefers traveling and taking a vacation once or twice a year. Any extra money you have after your needs are met can be dedicated to travel.

Some people may prefer to dedicate their money to their pets, others may want to invest in the stock market, while others may be thinking about becoming an entrepreneur. Your discretionary money can pretty much be dedicated to anything that you think is important and can enhance your life.

Which Budget Is Right for You?

As you can see, there are several different ways to budget for your future. While the end-goal is the same with all of them, only one will fit with your lifestyle and your way of managing money.

To decide which system will work best for you, there are a few things you need to keep in mind.

- How much time do you have to monitor your budget? Some methods are relatively easy and do not require a lot of detailed record-keeping. But others may require elaborate record-keeping with numerous Excel spreadsheets and constantly tracking every penny you spend. If you don't have a lot of time to dedicate to such extensive record-keeping, you might want to start working a budget that has a little more give and take.

- You should also think about how often you should monitor your budget. Those who are pretty confident that their budget is on the right track might review their results on a monthly basis, while others may choose to view it once or twice a year. If you're still trying to get the balance just right, you might be more inclined to review it on a weekly basis or even after every purchase.

At the very least, having a budget allows you to approach life with confidence. You know that you have a plan and a direction you want to go in. Every time you pay a bill, you get a sense of pride that you are one step closer to your goals, and that is worth money in the bank.

7 Ways to Make Budgeting More Enjoyable

There are many benefits to learning how to budget properly, but many of us are gun shy from those arduous days from our middle and high school classrooms. However, with just a few little tips, those boring math classes can be brought to life and you can find out just how much fun you can have crunching those numbers.

1. **Take Advantage of Modern Tech**

    If you really aren't good at numbers, take advantage of modern tech. There are plenty of excellent applications that can help you to get your budgeting done with minimal effort. Each one has its own set of features that can be applied to your situation. After a careful search and analysis of the available options, it is possible to find one that will fit your needs.

2. **Know Your Goals**

    The work becomes a lot more interesting when you know why you're doing it. When you start by establishing some clear-cut goals, even if they are small ones, it gives meaning to what you want to do. If you set both long and short-term goals, you'll have certain milestones to achieve and once you've mastered a few of them, you'll find yourself motivated to push forward.

Start by setting up a few easy ones that you know you can achieve, and then watch the magic as it happens. There is nothing more motivating and encouraging than success. The larger goals can be broken up into small steps. Each milestone you pass will help you to see that you are making progress even if the end is months or years away.

3. Give Yourself Rewards

The main reason we do anything is for the rewards. We go to work for the reward of the paycheck, we study hard in school for the reward of a good grade, we do our best in competition for the reward of the prize, and we struggle through relationships for the reward of a happy family life. It just stands to reason that you will work harder when there is something rewarding at the end of the fight.

There are all types of rewards you might give yourself, just make sure that your reward is in line with your goals. You could treat yourself to a night on the town after a completing a full month of budgeting, set aside a little money for a vacation or a weekend getaway, or reward yourself with a new outfit or a pair of shoes.

The main point is that you acknowledge what you have accomplished and be happy about it. Perfection is a good goal to reach, but if it is offered at the expense of your mental and emotional stability, you may reach your goal but there won't be much satisfaction in it.

4. It's Not Just About You

Even if you have small children, letting everyone in the family be a part of the solution takes a lot of the burden off of you and can make it much more rewarding. Some people turn budgeting into a game by allowing the children to compete by seeing who can either make the most money on odd jobs or who can save the most.

Just as rewards will work well for you, they'll do wonders to motivate the youngest ones in the family: a trip to the local candy store, something from the ice-cream truck, or a day at the park (that's free!). Remember, a reward for your kids is also a reward for you. It'll be easier to achieve your goals and it will be a major boost to your children's self-esteem. They'll learn good money managing habits and they'll feel like part of the solution rather than the problem.

5. Become More Self-Sufficient

Saving money is not just about shifting dollars from one place to another. While you can save that way, it is a lot more fun to learn creative ways to acquire the things you need without shelling out a lot of cash. There is nothing more rewarding than heading out to your backyard to pick your vegetables for dinner than finding them at your local supermarket.

And the best part of it is that everyone in the family can take part. Your children will learn a valuable and precious skill that will last them a lifetime, and you'll save money at the same time. Once they taste the difference in the foods you grow, they may not want to eat store-bought food ever again.

There are a lot of things you can do to save money. In addition to growing your own food, you can create your own cleaning supplies, learn to sew your own clothes, or even make your own hair products. In fact, if you do well, you may be able to parlay some of that into a side business that will help you to keep you on budget too. What can be better than that?

6. **Think Differently About Money**

   Learn to think of money in a different way. Chances are, you've seen money as a source of stress and anxiety for a while now. The need for money has caused many to fall so far into debt, it's no wonder so many people see it in a negative light.

   Now, as you begin to see your money working for you rather than against you, it is possible to view it as a means to an end. As you learn how to prioritize your spending and you see its effects as you pass one milestone after another, you'll see money more as a tool you can utilize to your advantage.

7. **Plan for Early Retirement**

   The sooner you start planning for retirement, the sooner you'll be able to see money as a way to make it happen. Think about all the things you can have if you are able to retire early. The time you can spend with your family, the vacations you'll enjoy, the time you'll have to do the things you love, and the stress-free life you will lead.

While budgeting may be a necessity, it doesn't have to be painful or stressful. By coming up with creative ways to make it more interesting, you can ensure your success. Creative budgeting can be a great way to motivate your whole family, friends, and neighbors to help you to achieve your goals without losing your heart in the process.

7 Important Steps for Building Good Credit

Bad credit can be the bane of anyone's existence. It can prevent you from renting a decent place to live, stop you from purchasing a home, cut off your means of education, and it might even be the reason you couldn't get a good job. If you have bad credit, then you already know what this feels like.

It can be very exciting to get that first credit card. Every purchase you make, every late payment, starts to develop into a picture that becomes very hard to erase. Being able to use credit responsibly is one sure way of securing your financial future.

Sadly though, this lesson comes a little too late for most people, and they end up having to rebuild their credit and recover from some painful decisions they have made in the past.

The good news though, is that no matter how bad your credit is today, there are ways to rebuild it and restore your good name. It may take time, but by applying some very basic principles you can establish a good credit history, one that you can be proud of.

Whether you're trying to restore your credit or you're just starting out, keep these little tips in mind to protect your image and make sure that your credit doesn't suffer from bad decisions in the future.

1. **Never Borrow More Than You Can Afford**

    You received your credit because you were viewed as creditworthy, so don't start off using it with bad spending habits. Make sure that when you use your card you only use it for things you can afford. It can be difficult to resist the temptation to buy things on credit that you can already buy without it, but it is a powerful signal to future creditors that you are being responsible. You'll be glad you were frugal when you can later get those big-ticket items you couldn't get before.

This is also true when it comes to taking out loans. Only borrow what you know for a fact you can pay back within a reasonable amount of time. Take a little time to look over your budget so that you know exactly what you can afford to pay on a monthly basis. If the loan payment amount exceeds that number, don't be afraid to walk away.

2. **Don't Use All of Your Credit**

Just because a creditor gives you a maximum limit, it does not give you carte blanche to use it all. When you max out your credit cards, creditors view it as irresponsible, especially if you're not in the habit of paying off your bill in full every month. Lenders notice that borrowers who max out their credit are usually the same ones that have difficulty paying off their balance. Try to keep your balance at around 40% of your credit limit to maintain a good credit score.

3. **Don't Get a Lot of Credit Cards**

Opening up too much new credit too soon can be very damaging to your credit.
Try sticking to only one credit card at a time. Establish a good rating with that one and use it for a couple of years before trying to apply for a new one. Your credit rating will remain strong if you don't race out of the gate but start building it up slow and steadily.

4. **Pay Your Balance in Full Every Month**

You've probably heard that it's important to pay your balance in full every month. If you are only charging what you can afford to pay, this is not a problem. When you are careful with your spending and can pay off your balance each month, you show your creditors that you are responsible. As a result, you'll end up with a higher credit score.

5. **Pay on Time**

One of the most important things you can do when it comes to paying your bills is to *pay on time*. It is important to make it a habit to pay everything on time so that it doesn't have a chance to negatively affect your score. Any bill that has the possibility of becoming delinquent and end up being sent to a collection agency can harm your credit.

6. **Manage Balances Properly**

There will be times when you have to carry a balance on some big-ticket items. If you find that you can't pay the balance in full at the end of the month, make sure that you pay a significant amount so that you are paying more than interest payments on the debt owed.

Always try to pay more than the minimum payment each month until you pay your balance down. When you do that and keep your balance owed to less than 30% of your credit limit, you protect your credit and can maintain a relatively high score.

7. **Allow Your Accounts to Mature**

Having good credit can be a good thing, but the longer you have it, the better. As your accounts mature it looks good on a credit report. When you keep the oldest accounts active, they give your credit image a boost. Keep in mind that if you close any account, it may take several years before it drops off of your record, so leave them open, even if you don't plan to use them. This will show creditors that you are not relying on it to get by.

Establishing good credit is extremely important for anyone who is seeking financial freedom. While there are several ways to reach that goal, establishing a good budget, and sticking to it is a surefire key to success. But budgeting doesn't have to mean months of drudgery and deprivation as some people have been led to believe. If you do it the right way, find a plan that works well with your lifestyle and personality, you're well on your way to discovering the freedom that comes from managing your money well.

It's not enough to have a good budget; you need to know how to implement it properly. That includes knowing how to use credit wisely. Setting up a good financial future, should not feel like a punishment, but should feel uplifting and rewarding. By following these very basic guidelines you can find success along the way and the big pay-off years down the line.

Chapter 3: Investing 101

Learning how to manage your money is a big step towards gaining financial freedom, but once you've succeeded, you're only half-way there. The reality is that finding wealth and financial security rarely comes from good management of credit and savings accounts.

Those two features can put you in a better financial position, but they don't erase the fact that you still need to work for your money. A savvy financial planner understands that the transition from working for your money to having your money work for you is a huge step. To get your money to work for you means that you have to invest.

Types of Investments to Add to Your Portfolio

There are a wide variety of investment options available for anyone who is willing to take the risk. Understanding your level of risk tolerance can make a major difference in which investment tools you choose to make. When making investment decisions, you need to decide if you're willing to invest for the long haul or you want a quick return and make a short-term investment. For most people, the first line of investment options for the long-term are either in stocks or bonds, but there's a wide variety of options to choose from.

1. **Stocks**

In its most basic definition, a stock is a purchase of a small portion of a specific company. When you buy a share, you are actually buying a percentage of the business' potential earnings and assets. When a business sells shares in its company, it is doing so in order to raise capital to invest in its own operations. As an investor, you can buy or sell your shares to improve your own financial portfolio.

When the value of the stock increases, an investor can then sell his shares at a higher price than what he bought it for and make a profit. Another way to make money in stocks is by purchasing stocks that pay dividends. Dividends are distributions of earnings given out periodically to investors. You can choose to invest in dividend stocks or growth stocks.

With dividend stocks, you will receive a regular distribution of earnings without the need to sell your interest in the business. Dividends can be paid out monthly, quarterly, bi-annually, annually or on some other payment schedule. Most companies that pay out dividends are pretty well-established and in most cases are considered safe.

Growth stocks are also shares in companies that are expected to see a certain amount of growth. They don't pay out any dividends, so you don't get a regular payout for owning them. The only way to turn a profit with a growth stock is to sell your shares in the business.

There is a certain level of risk with both options. Dividend stocks are usually the preferred choice for those with a low-risk tolerance. Growth stocks are a little less predictable but that doesn't mean they are less stable. There are times when the profits from a growth stock can actually be more rewarding than dividends.

If you're thinking of investing in the stock market, it just makes sense for you to compare the two, learn your level of risk tolerance, and decide which type works best for you.

2. **Bonds**

When you purchase a bond, you are technically lending money to the issuer and will receive a certain amount of interest for allowing them access to your funds.

For the most part, bonds are believed to be much safer than stocks, but the possibilities for grand returns is rare. You also have an additional risk to worry about. Just like with any company that extends loans to others, there is always a risk of the borrower going into default. Government bonds are usually safer because they are backed by the "full faith and credit" of the United States federal government. Next to government bonds in safety are state and city bonds. Corporate bonds come with more risk but are considered to be the third safest choice.

Investors earn profit from regular interest payments from the borrower, which is usually paid once or twice each year with the principal being paid back on the maturity date. Bonds are fixed-income investments, which means the amount of the investment is fixed and does not change.

3. Mutual Funds

When you purchase a mutual fund, you are investing in a larger number of stocks with one single transaction. The funds collect money from a wide range of investors and then invest that money into select stocks, bonds, or assets.

These investment instruments are found and selected based on a set strategy. For example, one fund may only be a specific type of stocks or bonds, while others may have a different set of parameters. One fund may choose to work only with international stocks while another may want to focus on technology or the sciences.

Profits are made when the selected list of investments goes up in price. The money received could be in the form of dividends or interest. Periodically these are dispersed to the customer. Also, when the investments actually do increase in value, owners are free to sell their interest for a profit.

4. Index Funds

An index fund is one type of mutual fund which passively tracks all the stocks in a particular index. This type of fund doesn't use a fund manager to choose which stocks to invest in. Rather, the decision is based on all the stocks in that particular index. For example, one well-known index fund is the Standard & Poor's 500, which has the goal of matching the performance of the S&P 500 by holding shares in every one of the companies listed in that index.

One of the biggest advantages of investing in index funds is their low cost. Because there is no need to have a live person to manage the fund, you save money.

Index funds earn money through either dividend or interest payments made periodically. They can also make money when the value of their investment increases. Investors can sell their share in the fund when the price goes up.

5. Exchange Traded Funds (ETFs)

One type of index fund is an exchange-traded fund or an ETF. ETFs strive to copy the performance of a specific kind of index. Because they are also not actively managed, they are also much cheaper than mutual funds.

You can purchase ETFs on the regular stock exchange and sell them the same way. The price will fluctuate up and down throughout the day, just like regular stocks. However, both mutual and index funds have a fixed price that is only adjusted at the end of each trading day.

Profits are earned the same as with all other funds. Some ETFs pay dividends or interest rates, but you can also make money when the fund increases in value and you sell it at a profit.

6. Options

An option is simply a contract to buy or sell a particular stock at a pre-determined price or on a set date. Even though you enter into a contract, you are not required to buy or sell the stock, so you have the flexibility to decline the offer if you choose to. The contract only gives you an "option" to make such a transaction. You also have the option to sell the contract to another investor or let it expire.

An options contract allows you to lock in a particular stock at a lower price. If you are right, you are opting in on a chance to purchase the stock at a later date at a more favorable price than the rest of the market. If your predictions are wrong, you lose only the money you invested in buying the contract and walk away.

You will have to open a brokerage account with either your bank or an investment firm. Once the account is opened and funded, you can start making your investment.

However, you have to be very careful with the fees. Some firms will charge monthly fees while others will charge for every transaction. When calculating your profits, make sure that once you've made your decision, the profits you claim are not eaten up by the costs of making that transaction.

Understanding the Bond Market

Before you purchase a bond, you need to do a little research. There are loads of online resources that will help you to find the best bonds to invest in. Look for sites that will break down all of the information on the different securities, any news related to their performance, analysis, and other vital information that can help you to make a decision. Some of the most frequently used sites include Investopedia, Morningstar, Yahoo, and the Finance Bond Center.

As an individual investor, you cannot personally invest in the bond market. You will have to enlist the aid of an institutional investor. Most do this through their employee pension fund, their banks, an endowment fund, or an investment banker. If you don't have any one of these at your disposal, your next step would be to find an asset manager to make the investment for you.

There are three groups that are active in the bond market.

Issuers: Those that develop, register, and/or sell bonds on the market. These could be corporations or they could be from a governmental agency. We are probably most familiar with US Treasury bonds, which are issued by the Treasury Department, but there are other agencies that also issue bonds. Most bonds issued from the government will reach maturity after 10 years.

Underwriters: A group that evaluates the risks of each of the bonds. They buy securities from the issuers and then resells them to the buyers for a profit.

Participants: Participants buy bonds as loans to the various entities. The loans are extended for the length of the security and receive the face value of the bond once it reaches its maturity date.

Grades are issued by a bond rating agency and usually come in the form of a letter grade. For example, a "AAA" rating is considered very high quality and is least likely to go into default. A "BBB" rating is considered to be a medium risk, and anything that is a BB or lower is considered a high-risk investment opportunity.

Understanding the Stock Market

The stock market is where you buy shares in publicly traded companies. Like bonds, there are different types of stocks: common stocks, options, and futures.

The primary role of the stock market is to bring buyers and sellers together in a controlled environment. The market ensures that all securities are traded fairly, honestly, and with transparency. They keep trade between investors and corporations above board.

The stock market has two separate components. The first is set aside for new businesses offering initial public offerings or IPOs for trade. Underwriters set the initial price of securities for sale. IPOs tend to be higher risk investments as most of these corporations have not yet proven their worth.

The second component is for trading equities for the more established businesses. This is where the majority of trading on the stock market takes place.

There are several different stock exchanges, each one offering different securities to trade.

Nasdaq: This is an online electronic exchange that lists the securities issued from companies with a smaller capitalization. Stocks on the Nasdaq includes companies trading in a wide range of industries, including consumer goods, services, utilities, healthcare, and technology.

New York Stock Exchange: The NYSE trades some of the oldest and largest public companies in existence. You have probably heard of the Dow Jones Industrial Average (DJIA), which consists of the top 30 largest companies on the NYSE. These are also the oldest and most referred to indexes in the world.

American Stock Exchange: Initially, it was used for trading completely new asset classes. Today, it is the exchange used for buying and selling ETFs.

There are several distinct differences between the bond market and the stock market. The stock market has a central place of trade where investors of all sorts can buy and sell their interests, where the bond market does not. Also, there is a difference in risk levels between the two. Those who choose to invest in the stock market are likely exposed to a higher level of risk than those who invest in the bond market.

Bonds, however, are more likely to be affected by inflation and interest rates. When there is an increase in interest rates, the prices of bonds tend to drop. On the other hand, if the interest rates are high, the value of the bond itself can be deflated.

Credit risks are also something you need to carefully consider. Purchasing a bond from a company with a poor credit leaves you open to a potential default. In most cases, the issuer may not even be able to make the minimum interest payments on your investment and you could lose a lot more.

Some of the safest investment options to start with are US Treasury bonds. You are less likely to experience a default, but that doesn't mean they are 100% risk-free. They are still susceptible to price volatility over the life of the loan.

Tips on Choosing the Right Stocks for You

Your choice of stocks to trade will depend on several factors. 1) your experience, 2) how much you have to invest, 3) and your actual investment strategy.

There are several strategies to consider: day trading, position trading or long-term trading. It is important to note that your trading plan is not a fixed strategy, as it needs to be dynamic and flexible enough to adapt to a constantly changing marketplace. Later, as you begin trading and observing your successes and failures, you'll become wiser in your decisions, recognize your strengths and weaknesses and learn to utilize that new knowledge more effectively.

Before you begin:

1. Know your goals. What do you hope to accomplish with your financial portfolio? Those who are looking to generate an income will look at low-growth firms in stable industries like utilities, REITs (Real Estate Investment Trusts), and partnerships. If you have a clear picture of your risk tolerance and how you will manage it, you will be looking to preserve your capital by investing in premium blue-chip stocks.

2. If you're more interested in preserving capital, then you might focus your attention on those companies that go through various life cycle stages and ranging market caps.

3. All stocks will go up and down in price, but they won't all rise at the same time. By investing in a wider range of stocks, you'll have a better chance of generating a consistent amount of income with no significant downsides to deal with.

4. Be observant. When investing in stocks, you are always learning. Stay up to date on all current market events. Make it a habit to read blogs, study magazines, and keep abreast of the latest financial news. You should do this on a daily basis.

5. Finding the right company. Start by tracking the performance of a chosen industry and then look at the stocks listed in that industry. Check out the ETF for the industry and see what companies they are holding.

6. Filtering by sector or industry can be a good start, but you can expand the search even further and filter your list by other details like market cap, dividend yield, or other practical metrics that will help you to decide.

7. Don't waste your energy on trying to catch the absolute bottom of any stock price, nor should you try to stay in a trade until it maxes out at the very top. Keep your focus on growing your net worth and get out when you know it will be to your benefit.

8. Don't give in to FOMO, or the fear of missing out. View each trade as a learning experience and tap into the ones you can and forget about the ones you can't.

9. Choose only one stock to begin with and study the results over time.

10. Use trading charts to give you a clear understanding of the market and stock movements.

11. Follow through with your plan until you get the desired results.

Choosing Stocks That Fit Your Personality

We are naturally drawn to those things that we understand the best. If you are a young twenty-something and have spent your formative years playing lots of video games, you have a quick mind, and know how to stay focused, short-term investing may be the best strategy for you.

On the other hand, if you're nearing retirement age, are slow at making decisions, and like to look at things from all angles, then maybe day trading would be a better choice. If your goal is to generate a little extra income from one month to the next, then dividend trading might be your best option.

Whatever investment style you choose, think it through carefully. It is very important that you understand the stock's volatility, price movements, and expected performance.

Manage Your Risk

Every investment option comes with its own level of risk. Your goal is to preserve your capital and manage that risk with every decision you make. Even if you suffer losses, you want to be sure that you have enough capital left to keep something in play.

Every investment you choose should be an educational experience. Take the time to analyze and calculate the costs, striving to make an informed decision.

Don't Over Complicate It

Keep it as simple as possible. Every stock has its own set of habits and moves; the more you understand these habits — the easier it will be to anticipate how it moves and make decisions accordingly. Once you feel comfortable with one stock, add another, and repeat the process. If you continue this pattern, you are less likely to find yourself in over your head.

What Is an Investment Plan?

Basically, it is a plan of how you will invest in the stock market. It dictates your actions so you don't make impulse decisions that can put your capital at risk. Here is a sample Day Trading plan you can start with until you get your feet wet:

1. Trade one stock at a time
2. When I am familiar with that stock, I will invest in a second one.
3. Trade only within the $20–$40 price range
4. Trade stocks that have an average 30-day volume that ranges a minimum of 1 million shares and a maximum of 2 million
5. The stock should have a medium degree of volatility
6. No trading in biotech stocks
7. I will max my portfolio at five stocks
8. I will study each of the stock's performance during multiple time frames every night
9. I will follow S&P Futures

Here is a sample plan for swing trading

1. Select up to 50 stocks for trade
2. Invest in one at a time
3. When I am comfortable and familiar with one then I will add another
4. The price will be $25 or more
5. Stocks will have an average 30-day volume of 500,000 shares a day or more
6. I will choose 25 for a long watch list

    a. Each will have increasing revenues and earnings
    b. They will have high relative strength in its leading sectors
    c. They will be above the 200 moving average
    d. They should be following the S&P Futures

7. I will choose 25 for my short watch list

    a. These will have declining revenues and earnings
    b. They will have a low relative strength in the leading sectors
    c. They will perform below the 200 moving average
    d. They should be following the S&P Futures

8. I will study the stochastics signal

The 5 Best Stock Trading Strategies of All Time

Once you've decided on the company to invest in, you're probably eager to get started making money. You need a strategy that dictates just how you want to invest. There are five different strategies for investing in stocks, and it pays to understand a little about each of them to help you determine how you will invest your money.

General Trading: You are anticipating the moves of the overall market, looking for averages that will give you an idea of their direction.

Selective Trading: Selective trading means you will pick out stocks which you expect to perform better than the overall market over the course of the next year.

Buy Low Sell High: Enter the market when the prices are at an extreme low. If you choose well and the stock recovers, you can make a pretty tidy little profit.

Long-Pull Selection: Choose the businesses you expect to prosper over the long-term and will fare better than the average business within their industry.

Bargain Purchases: Choosing stocks that you know are selling below their market value.

Your approach to investing should not be based on impulses but should be thought out rationally, then applied with deliberate discipline. This way, you won't find yourself fretting over every change you see in the market but will be comfortable with your decisions and can understand the movements when they happen.

8 Worst Investing Mistakes to Avoid

When you do things deliberately, you're protecting yourself and your finances. However, new investors often give in to the powerful urge to take a chance on that one risky investment. That and several other mistakes are often at the heart of major financial losses in the market. Learning to avoid these can make a huge difference in how fast you build your portfolio and put you on the right track towards greater profits.

1. ***Investing Before You Understand.*** If you are not well-versed in one industry, you should avoid those stocks. Endeavor to understand the business model and how it plans to increase its profits. Always strive to get a clear picture of where the business is going and how it plans to get there before you commit.

2. ***Allowing Your Love of a Company Overshadow Good Judgment.*** Sometimes we fall in love with a company that is doing very well on the market. Never forget your goal is not to support a company that you love but to make money. While the stock may be doing well, its fundamentals can change at any time, so always keep abreast of what's happening with your stock and events that could impact it. Never love a stock so much that you can't sell it.

3. ***Failing to Exercise Patience.*** It is always wise to exercise patience when investing; the slow, deliberate movement often pays off better than those fast bursts to the top. Your expectations should be realistic so that you're not discouraged when things don't happen quickly.

4. ***Jumping in and Out of Trades too Often.*** While you may make a profit here and there, frequent trades incur frequent fees that will usually eat up any profits you make. Add to that the taxes you will have to pay later, and you could easily end up losing a boatload of money rather than boosting your bottom line.

5. ***Trying to Time the Market.*** Your chances are more likely to meet success from making informed decisions rather than trying to hit the market at a specific time.

6. ***Trying to Get Even.*** If you experience a loss in the market, it is best to walk away rather than wait for an opportunity to regain your money. Holding onto the stock could see you losing even more money as the price continues to slide. It is better to preserve at least some of your investment by selling your position and reinvesting what's left in a more stable option.

7. ***Not Diversifying.*** Always invest in more than one industry. This spreads your exposure over a wide range of possibilities and protects your assets. Try to allocate funds to all major sectors and avoid spending more than 10% of your portfolio into one single asset.

8. ***Making Emotional Decisions.*** Keep a cool head and let your logic govern your decisions. Keep your focus on the long-term results and the averages. It will keep you sane in this business and prevent you from making hasty decisions that could cost you in the long-run.

9. **Create an Action Plan.** Never try to beat the market, but always work towards your personal goals. Be realistic about your expectations and avoid jumping into a stock that makes promises that you know are too good to be true.

10. **Make Your Plan Automatic.** Once you put your plan into action, keep adding to it. Building your investment should continue on throughout your life.

11. **Take Advantage of Your Profits.** There is nothing wrong with skimming a little of your money off the top to enjoy right now, today. Perhaps at the end of the year, you can take 5% of your profits for a little fun. This will give you the incentive to keep pushing forward towards your goals and growing your portfolio.

No doubt, you will make mistakes when you invest in the stock market. Get used to it. It is a major part of investing. However, you can minimize the number of mistakes you make by following these basic guidelines. They will help you to become a better investor over time. By making decisions based on actual facts and data rather than emotions, you will be one step ahead of every other new investor that enters the market.

Chapter 4: Dividend Stocks

How would it feel if you could have a steady stream of income coming in on a regular basis without having to lift a finger to work? Most of us have dreamed about that happening, but some have actually been able to find it through dividend stocks. When you invest in dividend stocks, you are essentially building an ongoing income that will last as long as the company you invest in remains profitable.

However, before you drop all of your money into these stocks, you need to learn just how the dividend system works. How dividends are paid, and the different types of dividends you can choose. You probably enter this arena knowing that dividends are paid on different stocks but understanding how to find and capitalize on cash dividends, stock dividends, and property dividends can make all the difference in how well your investments perform. Here are some basic tips that will help you to enter this type of investment opportunity without making costly mistakes along the way.

When a Company Pays Dividends

Not all companies that earn a profit pay dividends. Some choose to hold onto their profits and then reinvest them back into the business, either by reducing their debt or expanding their operations. Companies that pay out dividends are literally sharing a percentage of their profits with their shareholders. Those who choose to invest in dividend stocks usually have the ultimate goal of using those regular payments to support themselves.

Before a dividend is paid out, it has to first be approved by the company's Board of Directors. If the company pays out monthly, then they have to have approval every month. Once the dividend is approved, there are three dates that an investor needs to know.

Declaration date: the date the company makes a public announcement of its decision to pay a dividend.

Ex-Dividend date: the date the decision is made as to who will be paid. Any shareholders on record on that date will receive a dividend for each share they own.

Payment date: This is the date the dividend is actually distributed to the shareholders. Most dividends are paid out quarterly, but there are several that pay monthly, bi-annually, or annually as well.

Visiting sites like Dividend.com will tell you how often dividends are paid for each stock and how much. For example, if you see a company is paying out $1.00/share every quarter, it means that investors are receiving $.25/share four times a year, not $1 four times a year.

Different Types of Dividends

The most common form of dividend payments is cash dividends. These are paid directly from the profits generated over a period of time. There are several different types of cash dividends. If you own preferred stock, then the company must make those dividend payments preferred shareholders first, before any payments are paid out to common stockholders. Preferred stock dividends are automatically set but common stock dividends can be changed, suspended, or even stopped completely based on the discretion of the Board of Directors.

1. **Property Dividends.** Some companies prefer to give property rather than cash to their shareholders. Property can take any form depending on the holdings of the company. A property dividend could be anything from pencils to gold to cars to salad

dressings. These are recorded at market value on the declaration date.

2. **Special Dividends.** Occasionally, a company may choose to make a special dividend for various reasons. These are usually one-time distributions that follow a major success in the business. Perhaps they won major litigation in court, they sold a portion of the business, or they successfully liquidated an investment. These special dividends can be either cash, additional shares in the company or property.

3. **Stock Dividends.** Stock dividends are when an investor receives additional shares in the company rather than a cash distribution. There are a number of reasons why a company may choose to issue shares this way. They may not have enough cash on hand to pay out a cash dividend, or they are trying to dilute the value of the stock to encourage more investors to begin trading. Lowering the price is an excellent enticement to invest. With more shares in the market, the value per share drops. It is a lot easier for investors to pay for a $10 share than one that's $100.

4. **Stock Split.** A stock split is very similar to a stock dividend. A company may opt to double, triple, or quadruple the number of outstanding shares. With a stock split, the value of each share is lowered, but each investor still has the same overall value of his investment. If you owned 100 shares at $100 each and the company offers a 2-1 stock split, you now own 200 shares at $50 each.

Whether or not dividend investing is right for you depends on your goals. When a company decides it is going to pay out dividends, one of the first things it considers is its ability to reinvest the cash it has on hand at a higher rate of interest than the shareholders could. For example, if a company you're investing in is earning 25% on its equity and they have no debt hanging over their head, management could decide to hold all of its earnings confident that the investor will not find another company that is able to bring in that much of a return.

From the investor's perspective, you might be only interested in investing in that company for the dividend to cover your living expenses. These types of investors are not necessarily interested in the actual value of the shares, but in whether or not you're going to be able to pay your bills with the dividends you earn.

The Payout Ratio

The payout ratio is the percentage of net income a company pays out as a dividend. It is important to understand this ratio when choosing which stocks to invest in. This percentage gives you the projected growth of a company and what you can expect from it going forward.

To calculate the payout ratio, look at the company's cash flow statement. For example, if a company's statement says that it paid out $2.166 billion in dividends to shareholders and its income statement says that it had a net income of $4.347 billion, you could calculate the ratio using the following formula.

$2,166,000,000 dividends
$4,347,000,000 net income

The answer 49.8% gives a pretty revealing figure. It shows that the company paid out nearly half of its net profits to shareholders over the year.

The Dividend Yield

Another box you will see when you look up a company's dividend history is the dividend yield. This tells you just how much you are earning in relation to the price of a share of a common stock at the current market price. When you buy a stock that has a high dividend yield, it can generate a nice source of income.

To calculate the dividend yield, divide the annual dividend by the current share price. So, if you were to invest in Starbucks today, your dividend yield would be calculated like this.

$1.44/94.16 = 1.53%

Dividends and Your Taxes

Dividends are taxed at a lower rate than your regular income taxes. Some dividends referred to as "qualified dividends" can be taxed at a higher rate in line with a capital gains tax. To avoid falling into this trap, in order for your dividends earned to be included in that lower rate tax bracket, you must hold the stocks for a minimum of 60 days.

Choosing Stocks That Pay High Dividends

When choosing to invest in dividend stocks, you want to find those that pay the highest of dividends. There are thousands of stocks that pay dividends, so you should be careful to examine each one closely. Look for those companies that have a history of steadily increasing dividends over at least twenty years. Analyze the company's past record until you are confident that they are in a position to continue this trend for the foreseeable future.

Keep in mind that a company's ability to pay dividends is directly related to its cash flow. You are looking for stability. A company can report a net loss and still have a healthy cash flow. If a company is lowering its dividend, you can bet that it's going to lose some stability as investors start to pull out. They will not lower their payout for a problem that they expect to be only temporary. On the other hand, a company that increases its dividend will only do so if the business is capable of maintaining the higher rate for an extended period of time.

DRIPS

As you start to earn dividends, the amount of money you receive may seem miniscule at best, but that's okay. Unless you need a healthy stream of cash flowing in, you can turn around and reinvest that money into buying more stocks through a Dividend Reinvestment Plan (DRIP).

When you enroll in a DRIP plan, you will no longer receive dividend payments, but the money will automatically be used to buy additional shares of the same stock. There are several reasons why you would want to do this:

- The small earnings will automatically be reinvested.
- Most DRIPS plans have minimal or no commission fees
- You are allowed to purchase fractional shares, which over time can increase your wealth significantly.
- You can split your dividend repurchase plan, so you still receive some cash payout while the rest of the money goes to purchase additional shares.

Remember, for every share you purchase, the dividend payout you receive will increase, but with DRIPS, you won't be putting any more of your working capital into the account, and the investment will begin to pay for itself.

Think of how this could work to your benefit. Imagine owning 1,000 shares of a company valued at $49 per share. The annual dividend payout is 1.50/share paid out quarterly. You would receive a quarterly payment of .375 for each share or $375.00. You could receive all of that money each quarter with no problem, but if you don't need the cash to cover living expenses, then you could enroll in DRIPS and reinvest all of it (or some of it) to purchase additional shares of the same stock. $375 could buy you another 7 shares. The next time a dividend payout is due, your income would have moved from $375 to $377.62.

If you continue to repeat this pattern over the next 10 to 20 years, you could see how this would increase your earnings without you ever having to put another dime in the pot. DRIPS is giving yourself a raise.

How to Find the Best Dividend Stocks for Your Portfolio

In order to generate enough of an income from dividends, most people invest in high dividend stocks. When you make good choices and consistently contribute to your portfolio, you can generate quite a passive income that you can live off of during your later years. The most successful investors build up a portfolio based on higher dividend payouts.

There are several ways to find these stocks, but you have to be careful. Often looking at dividend yields can be deceiving, so you need to always be conscious of a possible dividend trap. You need to find those high dividend stocks and still give yourself some type of protection against potential risks where dividends could be cut or eliminated.

- The payout ratio should not exceed 70%, which means that the company is retaining a minimum of 30% of its earning to reinvest.
- Look for companies with a good pricing flexibility. That way, they can raise their prices if the inflation rate becomes too high.

This keeps the money flowing into your bank account, even if the economy is not stable.
- Look at the debt-to-equity ratio of the company. It should be 50% or less. This tells you that there is a $1 of net worth to every $1 of debt the company holds.
- The P/E ratio should be 15 or less, which can provide some protection just in case the dividend is cut for some reason.

Do Not Make These 10 Dividend Investing Mistakes

Buying dividend stocks can be tricky. While the potential for profit is great, you can easily fall into huge pitfalls if you're not careful in your search. Don't be hasty in making a decision. Still, with a little knowledge you can avoid many of the mistakes often associated with these kinds of investments.

1. **Don't Trust a Hot Tip.** It doesn't matter how much you trust the person giving it, a tip is only a tip. You can trust someone's sincerity but make it a rule to always verify the information you receive. At the very least, you should look up the company's statements over the last year or two and run the numbers yourself. Look under the hood, kick the tires and so on. Check to see if any insiders are buying shares or if possible, talk directly with someone in the company who may know what's in line for the future.

2. **Do the Work.** Yes, doing the research can be a real pain, but it will pay off in the end. Always do the homework. This will help to keep you from being too emotionally invested in a potential stock. When you understand what you're buying and know how the company is being managed, you're less likely to make an impulse decision that you might regret later. If the

market takes a dive, you will know exactly why and already have a back-up plan to cut your losses.

3. ***Don't Buy/Sell for the Dividend Alone.*** Don't buy the stock just to get the dividend and then sell it right afterward. You'll lose money. Yes, you will collect the dividend as promised, but in most cases, the price of the share will drop considerably after the payout. At the very best, you can expect to break even. Investors rarely make money on this type of trade, and much of what you earn will be eaten up with fees and commissions.

4. ***Look Beyond the Yield.*** Just because a stock has a high yield doesn't always mean that it's not in trouble. Don't be blinded by a high yield to convince you that a stock is worth it. Some companies that have a low yield are far steadier and more reliable than those with a volatile history and a high yield. Always look at the big picture before making a decision. You want to know why the yield is high. Is it because it pays high dividends or because of its low share price?

5. ***Look to the Future.*** When you research a stock, you are looking at either its history or where it stands in the present. This is important because it gives you a real time picture of what you can expect from the company. Your goal is to generate a passive income that you can rely on in later years so you also need to know what to expect in the future.

If you are smart, you will look at the company's history to see how well it has performed in the past and use that information to project into the future. If they have historically raised dividends periodically in the past, it might be reasonable to believe they will continue that trend, especially if the numbers look good. Keep a watchful eye out for any news that could have an impact on the company's development or other issues that may not be readily apparent.

6. ***Always Keep a Watch on the Market.*** Don't assume that because you've invested in a company that has a solid history, good numbers, and has hit all of your earmarks, that you should just let everything ride. Even the big stable companies will one day come crashing down. Of the thousands of companies that were on the NYSE 100 years ago, less than two dozen remain. That means that even the massive conglomerates of the past have one day crashed and burned. Always keep a close eye on the market. It's the only way to protect your investment.

7. ***Buying a Stock Based Solely on the Price.*** There is a huge difference between a share price and its actual value. You need to understand this difference. Just because a stock has a low price and appears more affordable doesn't guarantee that it's a good deal. Buying based purely on price is not investing, it is merely gambling, which doesn't yield the kind of results you need to build up a portfolio.

8. ***Keeping a Bad Stock for Too Long.*** When a stock is performing poorly, dump it. That stock is not your friend; it's not someone you owe anything to. If the price is plummeting and there is no indication that it is going to recover anytime soon, waiting to sell is almost a guarantee that you're going to lose. Get rid of it, don't let emotions dictate what you should do; there are thousands of other options that will earn you money. If the stock does recover later on, you can always buy back in.

9. ***Don't Forget Your Taxes.*** Too often, investors get wrapped up in their earnings and fail to account for the debt they owe to Uncle Sam. Anytime you are earning money, there will be

taxes to be paid. No matter what investment tool you use, if you're not sure of your tax obligations, talk to a tax accountant and play it safe. You should do this every year, because tax laws change frequently. You will need to adjust your investment plan to ensure that your earnings are more than enough to keep the IRS at bay.

10. ***Taking the Media Too Seriously.*** When you start to research different stocks there will be an endless stream of media reports, financial analysts, and opinions about what is a good or a bad stock. Many of them have very good information to consider but they are not always right. The value of their information is only as good as their resources. No source is 100% reliable. Always do your best to verify any information you receive, especially if you are not getting it directly from the company itself.

Choosing the best high dividend stocks is not rocket science, but it can make you feel like you're navigating one the craters on the moon. There are so many dark areas where you can get into trouble, you will have to be extra careful not to fall into any of the traps that catch so many novice investors.

What You Need to Know About Dividend Tax Rates

As your profits start to roll in, it is important to keep everything in perspective. As much as you'd like to think so, all of that money is not yours. As usual, Uncle Sam is sitting on the sideline waiting for his share. Once you start collecting dividends, you'll have to set some of those proceeds aside to keep him appeased.

Most dividends are paid in the form of cash but depending on where you decide to put your investments, you may also receive them in the form of additional stocks, stock options, property, services, or options.

No matter what instrument you invest in, it is considered profit, and you must claim it on your income taxes.

Ordinary vs. Qualified Dividends

There are two different types of dividends you might be receiving. Ordinary dividends are those received from the profits of a company. The amount you receive is usually based on the type of stock you have. Preferred stocks pay more than the common stock investments, but any dividend received from a preferred stock will still be considered an ordinary dividend unless it is stipulated otherwise.

Qualified dividends meet the IRS's requirements for capital gains taxes, which are taxed at a higher rate than ordinary dividends. Depending on your tax bracket, you could expect to pay anywhere from nothing to as much as 20% of your income.

Under the current tax laws, you must report all dividend income received even if it is only a small amount. If you received more than $10 from any one company, you will need to file a Form 1099-DIV declaring the exact amount you received. If the dividends you received come from a trust, estate or an S-corporation, you should also file a Schedule K-1, which will determine the percentage of dividends that you must pay taxes on.

You should automatically receive the required forms you should file from the company, but if for some reason you don't, you are still required to report the income on your tax return. Even if you don't receive an actual payout of those dividends, the IRS still sees them as taxable income. So, even if you reinvest them into purchasing more stocks, you are still required to report that as income.

How to Report Dividends

You can report your dividend income on your regular 1040 From. If your total income received amounts to more than $1,500 or if some of the dividends you receive are as a nominee for someone else, then you must also file a Schedule B form.

The thrill of seeing your money working for you can be truly amazing, but to ensure that those successes you receive are not dampened by trouble with the IRS, always take the time to file your income properly. This way, you can really enjoy the money you earn without reservation.

Chapter 5: Day Trading

If dividend investing is a little too slow for you, a faster way to get generate new cash is with day trading.

What Is Day Trading?

Day trading works the same as regular stock market investing, but all of your transactions are completed within one trading day. In essence, you buy and sell before the close of the trading day. Traders who make these types of trades are considered to be speculators, a form of trading that carries much higher risks.

One of the reasons for closing during a single day is to protect the gains investors might have received throughout the course of the trading day. Once the market closes, events can happen that could reverse the trend and they would be unable to manage things. A drop in prices can easily occur after the close of one day and before the open of the next and with that drop, much of their profits could go with it. However, by selling your position before the close of the day, you lock in whatever profits you have earned and thus cut your risks.

Day trades can be made in any market but are most commonly transacted in the stock or the foreign trade markets. Investors rely heavily on leverage for these short-term trading strategies, focusing on making their money on seemingly insignificant price movements.

As a day trader, you will need to keep abreast of any news events that may have an impact on the trades you're making. This strategy is called "trading the news" where you respond to economic statistics, interest rate movements, or corporate earnings. These types of events are subject to market psychology, and investors will react with quick but significant moves. Day traders anticipate these movements and take advantage of them to capitalize on their earnings.

While the risk can be very high, the attraction of day trading is the potential for amazingly fast and impressive profits. To get those though, you need to be a fast decision-maker, disciplined, and diligent enough to do the required research to improve your chances of success.

There are many reasons why you might want to try your hand at day trading.

- You can profit when the price is rising and when it is falling
- You get additional margin and can use the leverage and the quick movements in the market to capitalize on gains.
- While research is necessary, detailed research into a company's fundamentals is not necessary. You are tapping into small fluctuations so you don't need long-term investment strategies.
- You earn cash fast.

These are just some of the advantages of entering into day trading. If you think you have the fortitude and are a fast thinker, then the next step is to just pick a stock and start trading.

How to Start Day Trading

Day trading sounds simple enough, but there is definitely a learning curve. Picking the best stocks to trade is only the beginning. The most successful traders have become very skilled at applying what they call the "The Rule of the Three P's," Planning, Practice, and Patience.

Planning. You will definitely need a trading plan to get started. Develop a personal map to help you navigate your trades. You are entering a highly volatile market and things will be moving quickly. If you're not prepared, you'll miss your marks and end up losing more money than you'll gain.

Practice. You won't get it right the first time out of the gate. It might be best to practice with one of the online trading platforms that let you test out your theories before you actually put money in the game. The more practice you get, the better you'll be at predicting when many of these volatile movements will happen. If you don't get it right, don't let that discourage you. Some of the most experienced day traders miss out from time to time. Just keep trying until you hit your rhythm.

Patience. Once you have a good trading plan and you get started, you'll experience some ups and downs. You need patience enough to stick to your plan to the end.

A day trader knows the when, what, and how to trade every stock before he enters the market. To do that, you need to understand how to use volatility to your advantage.

Volatility is directly linked to the activity of short-term traders and reflects the dispersion of a stock's returns on the market index. It can be determined by the difference between a stock's high and lows for a given day and then divided by the actual price for the same day. But the fluctuation of the price is only one factor that measures volatility. For example, a stock with a $50 share price that fluctuates as much as $5 in a single day is considered to be a lot more volatile than a $150 share that also fluctuates in the $5 range. It is the percentage of the move that also factors into its volatility.

The best day traders look to trade the most volatile stocks. It is the most efficient means of making money fast. These stocks tend to offer the best profit potential, but they come with their own level of risk. If you're aiming to try your hand at one of these, you need two things:

1. Where to find the most volatile stocks to trade
2. How to trade them with technical indicators

The best way to find a volatile stock is to run a stock screen through a platform like stockfetcher.com. These sites use filters to track the most active stocks. For example, you can select stocks that average moves of 5% or greater between opening and closing on each of the last 100 days. You can also filter by stock prices as well.

For a more intensive search, another platform you can use is Finviz.com. Its free version will give you a list of the top gainers and the top losers in the market each day. You also have the option to filter the results further, looking for details on market capitalization, volume, and performance. You can be very specific in the type of filters you use so that you can end up with a list of stocks that meet very exacting parameters.

Nasdaq.com also lists the markets biggest gainers and loser, but their results are not filtered for volatility. Instead, you'll get a list of stocks that have the potential of being volatile. You'll need to manually sift through the list to see which stocks have the possibility of going volatile on a trading day.

Now to the question of how to trade them. When you have chosen your stock and are ready to make a trade, you need to be patient and wait for the precise moment to enter the market. One of the biggest advantages you will have is something called "directional bias." This is when specific indicators will be observed that tell you in which way the price is moving. You must always watch the price action to determine if the price is swinging high or low in comparison to previous waves.

The Stochastic Oscillator. Another useful tool you can use is the stochastic oscillator for predicting volatile stocks. This filters for stocks that may not have a very clear trend. Even when a stock is volatile, it can fall into a range before taking off in either direction. Just one single move can quickly change things, so the best thing to do is to hold off until you get confirmation that a price is going to reverse in one way or another.

In such cases, the price may not have a clear-cut direction, but may simply be moving sideways for a time. The best investment strategy is to wait until the price moves above 80 and then falls again. That's when you sell close to or at the top of its range. You can place your stop directly above the new high and your target at 75% of the total range. So, if the range has a high of $1, place your target at $0.25 over the low.

At the bottom, you can establish a long position if the stochastic falls below 20 and begins to rally above it. Place your stop underneath the new low and your target should go 75% up from the bottom. Again, if the range has a high of $1, the target can be at $0.25 below the high.

With the stochastic oscillator, make your trades when they hit 80 and above for uptrends and 20 or below when they are in a downtrend. You will have to move quickly though. If it is truly in a trend, even a delay of one minute could move the price too far away from your target to make any worthwhile trade.

When you are in a trade, ignore signals that may say contrary to what you believe. Let the trade play through. It will either hit the target or the stop.

Volatile stocks are a great way to earn fast money if you have the stomach for it. If you can successfully identify a trend, you will have access to even greater profits. Just follow the directional bias in order to help you make your decision.

Keep in mind that just because a stock is volatile, doesn't necessarily mean that it will trend. Prices can move back and forth sideways for long periods of time. When you see that stochastic reaches either the 80 or 20 mark and then pulls back, it is an indication of a good opportunity to enter the trade.

Day Trading Strategies

There are no hard and fast secrets to successful day trading. While it can be extremely lucrative, it is full of potholes that could cost you just as much, if not more money than you can make. The secret is to develop a well-thought-out plan that you can follow to the letter. The problem with this is that most newbies do not fully understand the game, nor do they have any idea how to create such a plan. Here are just a few tips that can help you develop a good day trading plan to launch you into the market.

1. ***Never Stop Learning.*** The more knowledge you have, the less likely you will make a costly mistake. When you day trade, you need to be aware of all of the latest news in the market. You want to know anything that could happen that might have an impact on the stocks you're investing in. Never shrink back from doing the extra work, it will pay off in the end. This is even more important when the news is directly related to stocks, you're planning on investing in.

2. ***Have an Investment Fund Ready.*** Know exactly how much money you are willing and able to put at risk for every trade you plan to make. On average, day traders usually put up approximately 1-2% of their portfolio into day trades. Some only a half percent. Once you know that amount, portion it out

to the stocks you're willing to invest in, but know that there is always a risk, so never put up more than you can lose.

3. ***Make Sure You Have Time.*** Day trading takes time. Because you will have to constantly be watching the movements of the market, it could consume an entire day. If you don't have the time to dedicate to the process, it is better for you to find other ways to invest your money.

4. ***Start Small.*** Don't try to tackle too many stocks at once. When you're beginning, you need to get the feel for the market. Start with only one stock and when you gain your confidence increase it to two. Some even start smaller than that with buying fractional shares rather than a whole single share. Some brokers like Stockpile, will allow you to buy a small percentage of a share, so you can invest in higher-priced stocks without putting a whole lot of money at risk.

5. ***Stay Away From Penny Stocks.*** The tendency for newcomers is to look at the cheapest stocks on the market. Penny stocks are those stocks that are usually priced at $5 or less per share. On the surface, this looks like a great stock to start with, but penny stocks are questionable at best. The chances of getting a windfall from them is minimal. Most stocks that are trading below $5 a share have often fallen to the Penny Stock list because they have been delisted from the major stock exchanges and are already in trouble. Unless you see very clear signs of a reversal, your best bet is to stay clear of these seemingly good bargains.

6. ***Timing is Everything.*** Learn the timing of the market so you know when it's time to jump in. For example, many investors may place an order overnight for the next business day. This means that as soon as the market opens, those orders will be

executed so you will see a lot of movement during the first hours of trading, but that is not always a clear picture of market movement. It might be best to wait an extra half an hour until all those orders settle down Usually, the middle of the day is the less volatile with activity increasing the closer you get to the closing bell.

7. ***Take Advantage of Limit Orders.*** Market orders are placed at the best price offered at that specific time. They are not necessarily the best price for you. Limit orders, however, guarantee that the order will only be fulfilled at the price you set. If the price you set is not available, the order will not be filled. Limit orders give you the opportunity to place an order and know exactly the price you will pay.

8. ***Be Realistic.*** No one will win all of the time, but that doesn't mean you can't turn a profit. Your goal is to make more money than you lose. If you keep your limits within a set percentage of your account and plan your entry and exits accordingly, then you have a good chance of gaining more profits than losses, but you will have to stick to your plan and follow through on it.

9. *Never Lose Your Cool.* There will be those days when you won't have any idea what the market is doing. On those days, keep your emotions at bay. Always make decisions based on clear logic and reasoning, even if the market is not making any sense at the moment.

10. *Never Stray From Your Plan.* When you are day trading, decisions have to be made fast. That can be very difficult if you haven't done your homework. The price could catapult completely out of your reach while you're trying to figure things out. That's why it's so important to do your homework

before you enter the market, so you know the exact point to enter and exit. Creating a plan beforehand and relying on it as a guide is the secret to successful day trade. No matter what the numbers say, don't allow them to lure you into chasing profits but make sure that you follow the day trader's mantra – *Plan your trade and trade your plan.*

Making a Decision

Now that you have made a list of those stocks that are potential winners, you now have to decide which one to buy. A day trader usually looks at three factors:

- **Liquidity.** When a stock is liquid, you have room to enter and exit at a good price. Look for tight spreads between the bid and the asking price, or a low slippage price. The difference between what one would expect to pay for a stock and its actual price.

- **Volatility.** the expected price range within a single trading day. The more volatile the price the greater the chance for profits (or losses).

- **Volume.** How many times a particular stock has been bought and sold within a set time period. When you see a volume increase in a stock, there is heightened interest, and you can expect some type of price jump.

Once you've decided what stocks to buy and your plan is set on when to enter the market, you need to decide when to sell. Ideally, you want to sell when the price hits your target, but that is not the only time you can exit.

- Scalping: selling as soon as you make a profit.
- Fading: selling after the price has made a rapid move upward.
- Pivots: selling at the highest price point of the day
- Momentum: selling after news releases or trending moves.

If you find that the interest in the stock is beginning to diminish, you should not hesitate to sell. You should give the same attention to exiting your trade as you do for entering it. Remember, it must be specific enough that you know when to execute it without much deliberating.

Charts

Another way you can determine when to enter the market is by reading chart patterns. Candlestick patterns can take up a whole book on their own. They provide a wealth of ways to look for an entry point. However, one of the most common is the doji reversal pattern.

1. Find a volume spike, which shows if traders are supporting this price level.
2. Find the support for that price. It could be the low or the high of the previous day.
3. Find the level 2 situation, which shows all open orders for that stock.

By following these basic steps, you should be able to anticipate when a price will turn around and offer more favorable positions.

Stop-Loss Orders

Stop-loss orders are meant to manage your losses. The order can be placed either in a low position or above a recent high to automatically sell when the price reaches that point. Using this will protect you from losing everything if the trade doesn't go your way.

Day trading is tricky at best. It is not something that you can get into blindly and expect to win. It takes skill, insight, and discipline. In time, with enough practice and determination, there is a very good chance that you will be successful.

Chapter 6: Real Estate Investing

Real estate opens a wealth of opportunities that one can parlay into a great fortune with the right tools. Unlike investing in the stock market, the principles behind real estate are pretty straightforward. But that doesn't mean that it will be easy breezy when you try to put them into action.

There are three ways you can make money from real estate.

- Increasing property value
- Rentals
- Investing in businesses that depend on real estate

In fact, the three options listed above are the most common ways to generate a nice passive income from the property you own. By learning just a few basic strategies to implement these, you could be well on your way to financial freedom.

Increasing Your Property Value

No matter what you do with your property, outside influences can still have a negative impact on its worth. Every decade or so, there seem to be occasions when the rate of inflation is expected to extend beyond the rate of long-term debt at the time. When that happens, you will find more people willing to extend themselves by borrowing money to finance a major property purchase. Then they sit back and wait for the inflation rate to go back up again. When it does, they can pay off their mortgage with a lower dollar value.

The key is to time the market just right. You need to know how to look at a project, analyze its price and timing, and decide if you will be able to create a good income that will be sufficient enough to support a higher valuation than what is currently evident.

Making Money From Rental Property

While rental property is not always as passive as it might seem, collecting rent is so simple anyone can do it. If you own any kind of property, you can simply rent it out to anyone who wishes to use it. It doesn't even matter what type of property it is; it could be a house, an apartment, or farmland. The money you get from their use of it can be quite lucrative.

As the owner of the property, it will be your responsibility to make sure that the property is being maintained in a usable condition. That means that you will have to be ever vigilant in repairs, supervision, and handling the negative aspects of undesirable tenants. You'll have to be insured against theft or other hazards and be proactive about possible concerns that may come up in relation to your property.

The good news though is that if you are a savvy property owner, there are ways to manage all of those things and still make a tidy profit. There are tools that have been designed that can make property management much easier than it has been in years. One you will find very practical is a special financial ratio, the capitalization rate. To understand this rate and how it works, consider this situation.

If you own a property that is earning $100,00/year and its price is set at $1,000,000, you could apply this formula by dividing the earnings by the value of the house to get the capitalization rate.

$100,000 / $1,000,000 – 0.1 or 10%

You could immediately earn 10% on your investment if you chose to pay cash for the purchase.

You can think of this in the same way you think of stocks. The worth of any real estate property is based on the net present value of the cash it generates for the owner and the cash flow it generates in relation to the price paid for its purchase. In essence, rental income can become a hedge to protect you during economic and financial collapses.

Of course, not all real estate is the same; some will be better suited for generating rental income while others are not. When you make a purchase at the right price but also at the right time, and you can find the right tenant to fill the space, you need not fear any upcoming real estate collapse. You will be collecting a steady stream of rental checks that will carry you through. However, if you don't plan the whole thing right, you could find yourself collecting rents that are far below the market and be stuck in that drain until the market recovers.

Investing in Businesses That Depend on Real Estate

There are lots of businesses that rely heavily on real estate. Many of them, like hotels, provide special services to the public. Other property owners provide office space for businesses, and there are those that can take an empty field and provide useful parking garages for those who drive to the area. Car washes, vending machines, agriculture, and more, the list is endless.

The trick for entering this highly lucrative market is to learn just enough to get started, but not so much that you become overwhelmed. Most new investors learn through a trial-and-error process. In this process, they usually make costly mistakes that can lead them to regrets. However, a plan that will help you to avoid such missteps and get you on the path to passive income can save you a world of time and frustration.

Start Investing One Step at a Time

The steps listed below will help you to make your first initial steps in the real estate market. After you are confident you can carry them out, use them as a checklist to make sure that you don't miss anything crucial that could cost you later on.

Identify Where You Are Financially

Real estate is probably the fastest way to reach financial independence. It is usually the goal that everyone strives to reach. It is one of the best ways to generate enough income to support you financially. But to get to that point, you have to be in a good financial position; you need enough savings to start the ball rolling.

If after looking at your financial situation, you're not quite there yet, there are things you can do to get you there faster.

There are five fundamental stages of wealth:

Stage 1: Survival state – where you are just making enough money to get by. This is the stage where you begin to pay off your debts and get relief from your financial burdens.

Stage 2: Stability state – your finances are not getting worse and you're managing to get your bills paid, and what little you have left you can start saving.

Stage 3: Saver state – you can pay all your bills and have a little bit left over to build up a nice little nest egg.

Stage 4: Growth state – At this point, your savings is turning into a tidy sum that you can seriously consider investing. Your savings should now be generating enough interest that it's worth noticing. If you're reinvesting those earnings, you are starting to get your money to work for you.

Stage 5: Income – you are now in a position where the money you have set aside can generate income for you.

It is important to understand your financial position. Some real estate strategies we discuss later on will be more appropriate for certain stages than others.

Choose Your Investment Strategy

While real estate investing is pretty simple, you still need a business plan. It doesn't have to be detailed, but you need to have a clear idea of what you're going to do. Choose one single strategy that will help you move from the stage you are starting with to the next level. Make sure you build some flexibility into your plan so that you're not derailed by unexpected events. Here are just a few ideas to get your started.

- Lease a large home and sublet rooms to tenants to cover your expenses
- Offer to find good deals for other real estate investors for a fee
- Help buyers find property to invest in, learning the ins and outs of real estate in the process.
- Help landlords find good tenants for their empty spaces
- Become a building manager/superintendent for other real estate investors

These strategies work well for those who are in either the **survival or stability state**. Any of these strategies will allow you to generate extra income without having to shell out a large sum of cash in the process. At the same time, you'll learn everything about the industry without having to spend any extra time taking classes or studying up on the latest policies. It'll be like getting paid to learn.

Start Cutting Back on Your Expenses

If you're at the **saver** stage, then you can do all of the things in the previous stages, but you can also add a few more steps to the process. For one thing, you should start cutting down on your household expenses.

- Use the additional income to pay down your mortgage so you can eliminate your monthly payment.

- Flip your house while you live in it. When you sell it, you create tax-free savings that you can use to invest in other properties.

- Purchase a house that needs significant repairs, move-in while fixing it and then rent it out at a higher price later.

- Become a real estate wholesaler, which is basically collecting a finder's fee for matching the deal with the right investor. This works great for those who may be interested in flipping a house in poor condition or plans to use it for some other profitable purchase. Homeowners who are in jeopardy of foreclosure are more likely to be favorable to such a deal because it allows them to get out from under without having to lose everything.

If you are at the **growth** stage, you are ready to grow your net worth into something much bigger. This is the perfect stage for jumping into real estate. There are several ways you can do this:

- Flipping houses: this allows you to generate larger sums of cash to reinvest in other profits.

- Use your savings to pay all cash for property.

- Borrow from several different properties you already own and then pay them down quickly one at a time.

- Buy three properties but sell or rent two. The money from the rental can pay for your living expenses on the third.

- Do a property exchange. Under the IRS's tax-free property exchange you can use Form 1031 to put off paying taxes on any property you sell if you can replace it with a similar piece of property. It makes it possible for you to start small and then grow your portfolio without having to face the negative impact of paying federal taxes with each property you purchase. The process would look like this:

    - You need enough cash on hand for a down payment and closing costs
    - Buy a basic rental property
    - Rent the property and save a portion of the rental for a few years
    - Sell the property
    - Use the 1031 form to purchase another, larger property at a discount
    - Repeat

Use Your Retirement Account to Purchase Rental Property

By using your tax-free retirement accounts to invest in real estate, you can garner a lot more income to invest, and avoid paying hefty income taxes for your purchase. Self-directed accounts like IRAs, ROTH

IRAs, 401Ks allow you to invest those funds in real estate and defer the income taxes you would have otherwise paid.

Maximize Your Income by Utilizing Existing Equity in Your Investments

If you're already at the income stage, you can maximize the income you're generating by selling low-quality properties and buying better ones. You could refinance any of your existing debt and exchange it for fixed low-interest loans and save even more money.

These are just some suggestions for real estate investment strategies. Probably one of them will be more appealing to you than others. Perhaps you have ideas of your own that you would like to consider. The main point is that you have to start with a viable and workable plan to make a success in real estate.

How to Select a Target Market

Your next step would be to pick a target market. Whatever market you choose will have a direct impact on the kind of cash you can generate. Most people prefer to choose a market that is close to their home. It is more efficient and less stressful than investing in properties that are out of your physical reach.

This does not mean that you can't invest in properties far away; it is definitely possible, but you do need to weigh the costs. Whatever market you choose, you need to evaluate the potential carefully.

You also need to do a good market analysis of the area you're interested in. Study the region for employment opportunities, rent prices, and potential population growth. Check the area for the following:

- Is the area convenient?
- Walkability
- Crime
- Schools
- Public transportation
- Local laws
- Taxes
- HOAs
- Etc.

With the above criteria, you can determine if you will be able to work with your target market or if you need to find another location. Start your examination with the larger metropolitan area and then gradually narrow the research down to smaller areas to determine the best location.

1. *Identify Your Criteria for Investment Property*

Determine what you think is a good investment. Write yourself an investment profile that you can show to others. This could be used to generate possible leads to properties you may want to pursue. This list could include property locations, prices, or a specific niche.

Your profile should also have a projection for how much rent you can charge for a property. You might want to start with a basic property to get your feet wet. Choose something you can live in for the moment and then grow from there.

You can find the best land, the most perfect home, at the ideal price, but if it's in a poor location, you may not be able to resell/rent it or if you do, you may not be able to get much of a profit from it.

When you find what you're looking for, even if everything appears to be right, do a little research and check nearby listings in the area. You'll get a pretty good picture of what similar properties are selling for so you can make accurate projections about your potential profits.

Even if you know you're buying a fixer-upper, it is important to have the property inspected. Don't hesitate to ask questions. You need to know how much you're going to need to put into the property and still be able to turn a profit.

Finally, make sure that there is a good chance of turning a profit before you take action. Don't forget to calculate the mortgage rate, utilities, taxes, insurance, repairs, and upkeep. All of that will have a bearing on how successful you'll be with your first investment.

No matter what you do, if the deal doesn't feel right, don't be afraid to walk away. Holding out for the best deals is going to be one of your best secrets to success.

2. *Get Your Support System in Place*

Real estate is best enjoyed with others. While you may be the sole investor on a project, you will still need a team of experts to turn to. Contractors, designers, real estate agents, and advisors could just be the beginning of your list. A good team could be ready to pick up the slack when you get into an area where you lack knowledge and expertise.

3. *Set Up Your Financing Options*

Depending on your credit rating and your financial situation, your options can vary. Here are just a few resources you can tap into.

- Federal Housing Administration
- Veterans Administration
- Conforming Loans (Fannie Mae/Freddie Mac)
- Bank Loans
- Hard Money Loans
- Private Lenders
- Seller Financing

It can be tricky to choose the right lender, but this is where you can call on the advice from your team.

4. *Get Your Down Payment and Closing Costs Ready*

While you can launch your new business with other people's money, you need to have some money of your own to invest. In most cases, a down payment is required to even get the ball rolling. Some down payments can be as little as 3% of the purchase price. Closing costs can also vary. Even in the best of deals, you may need as much as $20,000 of your own cash on hand.

5. *Start Looking for Deals*

Finding the right property requires a lot of legwork. Good deals will not just mysteriously find their way to you, you're going to have to start looking under every rock and peering into every nook and cranny before you find the property that you know is right.

Your marketing budget can be launched with practically nothing, but if you have some money to put towards it, the process gets a lot easier. Here are just a few ideas that have proven to be effective marketing campaigns.

- *Free campaign:* Find an agent who will agree to send you leads based on your list of expectations.

- *Referrals and Networking:* For a little extra money, you can have business cards or flyers printed with your requirements so that people can contact you when they find something.

- *Do a Drive or Walk By*: Make it a habit to visit your target neighborhood looking for possible deals. For Sale by Owner signs can be quite promising, but you can also look for homes that have been vacant for a long time, appear to be in need of repair, or even have for rent signs posted.

- *Wholesalers:* Let real estate wholesalers find the deals for you. Contact a few of them and get their list of possible properties.

If you have a little extra money to spend:

- **Start a Direct Mail Campaign:** Create your own letters or postcards to send to property owners in your target market. You can find the names and addresses by paying a list company. Some of these lists can be very lucrative:
    - Absentee owner properties
    - Multi-unit property owners
    - Owner-occupied homes
    - Recent evictions
    - Delinquent property taxes
    - Expired real estate listings
    - Pre-foreclosure and foreclosure properties

- Estate and probate sales

  o **Use your online presence:** Utilize social media. Set up a dedicated page to your real estate marketing plans on sites like Facebook, LinkedIn, Twitter, etc. Create an online business card to let people know what you're looking for.

  o **Car/Yard Signs:** Invest in magnetic or vinyl signs for your car or yard.

  o **Advertising:** Online or print advertising can get to areas that are difficult for you to reach on your own. Use resources like Google Adwords and don't neglect marketing in local newspapers, magazines, and radio. These efforts are a little pricey, but with the right strategy, they can get you good results fast.

6. **Make a Schedule**

You will need to set aside time to dedicate to your real estate venture. Be realistic with how much time you have to spend. Set your priorities first and then commit to the schedule you've set.

10 Important Features of Profitable Real Estate

To ensure that the property you choose is going to be profitable, it must have certain features. Even if it is a wreck and appears to be ready for demolition, there are still certain things you need to be sure of before your investment will be worthwhile. Here are the 10 most important features any property should have.

A Good Neighborhood

A look at the neighborhood can tell you a lot about the type of tenants you will attract. A location near a university will attract a lot of students. A location outside of the urban area may attract more families with children.

Property Taxes

All properties have taxes that need to be paid. You need to know how much they are and if the owners owe any back taxes. You can find out everything you need to know about the taxes with a visit to the county or city assessment office.

School System

If you are going to rent to families, you'll need to know something about the schools in the community. Few families are willing to buy or rent a home in a community with substandard schools.

Crime

Check with the local police department or visit the local library to see the latest crime statistics for the neighborhood. Pay extra attention to figures related to petty crimes, vandalism, and serious offenders.

Job Opportunities

Your best bet is to find properties in communities that are expanding their job market. These are more likely to attract buyers and renters to the area. Find out about job availabilities with the US Bureau of Labor Statistics. It can be a huge plus if major corporations are moving to the area. This kind of news often results in property values increasing as more people will be needed to fill those new jobs.

Neighborhood Amenities

What does the neighborhood have to offer? For children, there should be parks, playgrounds, movie theaters, etc. For adults, there should be fitness centers, public transportation, restaurants, and other entertainment venues.

Prospects for the Future

The city planning department should have information on any new developments that are proposed for the area. A lot of construction is a pretty good sign that the future is promising. However, be on the lookout for how those developments would impact property values.

Vacancies

When there are a lot of houses for rent or an excessive number of properties listed for sale, it could be a sign that the area is in a decline. Often when neighborhoods go into decline, property owners are forced to lower rents to keep their units occupied. On the other hand, when there are only a few vacancies in the area, you can comfortably ask for more rent.

Average Rent

If you're planning on renting, then you need to know just how much you can expect to get for a property in the area. You want to make sure that the rent will be enough to cover mortgage payments, property taxes, maintenance, and other forms of upkeep. Project these numbers into the future because what may be affordable today, could be marked out of your reach in five years, which may leave you forced to sell in an unfavorable market or go into bankruptcy later.

Exposure to Natural Disasters

It's not something that most people want to think about, but exposure to natural disasters can negatively impact your potential returns. Whether your home is in a flood zone, hurricane region, or earthquake-prone area, it's going to cost you either in insurance claims or direct repairs.

The best place to get reliable information is through government agencies, but don't stop there. The people in the community usually know everything about what's happening in the neighborhood. Talk to renters and property owners alike. Renters are more likely to give you a better picture since they have nothing to lose. They will tell you about any negatives you may not have thought of, but property owners will have a completely different perspective. If you keep these features in mind and your expectations realistic, you'll know when you've found the right property.

Top 15 Real Estate Investing Strategies

The strategies listed below are meant to give you an idea of the various ways you can generate your own income.

- **Flipping Houses:** Finding properties that need improvement, upgrading, or renovating and then reselling them at a profit.

- **Wholesaling:** Finding good deals on properties and then reselling them to a third party for an additional fee.

- **House Hacking:** Buy a multi-unit property and rent out the additional units. For example, buying a house and renting out the basement, or buying a duplex and renting out the extra unit.

- **BRRRR Investing:** Buy-Remodel-Rent-Refinance-Repeat. Buy a fixer-upper below market value, finance the property and then renovate. Refinance with a long-term mortgage and then take out your initial capital for a new investment.

- **The Cash Rental Strategy:** Buying property in cash. When you have completed the renovations and rented it out, you keep the majority of the money collected for yourself and can quickly invest in another property.

- **The Trade-Up Plan:** Using the IRS 1031 tax-free exchange to progressively trade up to bigger and better properties.

- **Hard Money Lending:** Giving short-term loans to investors who plan to fix-and-flip properties. Loans like these are usually given with high interest rates and up-front fees, so you'll make a good amount of cash in a short time.

- **Discounted Note Investing:** Buying real estate debt at a discount.

- **Syndications & Crowdfunding:** Pooling your money with individual investors to buy the perfect piece of property.

- **REITs:** Investing in companies that manage real estate. REIT stands for real estate investment trusts. You can buy REITs on the stock market, allowing you to own a small part of commercial real estate businesses and earn dividends on the profits in the interim.

Real estate can be a pretty lucrative business, but you have to be smart about it. There are many ways to achieve financial freedom through real estate, and each one has its own pros and cons. You can pick a strategy that works best for you or do several at a time. If one doesn't work right for you, then try another until you hit on your perfect match.

Chapter 7: Other Ways to Grow Wealth

The path to financial freedom can take you in many directions. Investing in the stock market and real estate are the most well-known entry points for new investors. They offer the lowest amount of risk in the investment world and give you a much better chance of success in the global marketplace.

That said, once you've gotten your feet wet and have acquired a taste for collecting passive money, you may want to start investing in other instruments that could prove to be even more lucrative for the private investor.

How to Start Investing in Exchange-Traded Funds (ETFs)

You've probably heard the term ETF mentioned in financial reports on the news and may not be sure of what it really is. You know it has something to do with the stock market, but you're not exactly sure about what they do.

ETFs or Exchange Traded Funds are groups of various investments that have been collected together to form one unit. These funds can be purchased on an exchange just like stocks with similar price movements.

Inside an ETF, you will find many different assets as opposed to a stock that will only be representative of only one asset. Because one share in an ETF covers so many assets, they are one of the easiest ways to diversify your portfolio. One ETF could possibly hold thousands of different stocks spread across several different industries.

Depending on the industries you may be interested in, you can purchase different types of ETFs.

- Bond ETFs consist of government, corporate, state, and municipal bonds.
- Industry ETFs can be compiled from stocks in a specific industry like banking, agriculture, or technology.
- Commodity ETFs would be a collection of different commodities like gold or oil.
- Currency ETFs include a selection of foreign currencies
- Inverse ETFs use the strategy of shorting various stocks. Shorting is the strategy of selling at a higher price and then repurchasing them after the price drops.

The only one on the list, the inverse ETFs are technically not exchange traded funds, but are actually exchange-traded notes or ETNs. These are bonds that are traded on the market like a stock and are banked by a bank.

Buying and selling ETFs

You can purchase ETFs through a broker. You have your choice of using either a traditional broker-dealer or an online broker. You can also use a robo-advisor, an automated investment system that uses certain algorithms to help you to build up your portfolio.

Advantages of ETFs

As an investor, you can buy or sell a wide range of these securities with one single transaction. This also saves you on commission fees as well. You might even find some brokers who offer no-commission trading on ETFs, cutting your costs even more.

Aside from saving on commissions, there are other ways ETFs can save you money. They cost very little to operate and manage. Because they are tracking an index, it is more passively-managed requiring far less time to govern, and since they are widely diversified, their level of risk is much lower.

Disadvantages of ETFs

There are some ETFs that have higher fees. These are the ones that are generally focused on one single industry, so your diversification is extremely limited. There are also some ETFs that are actively managed by portfolio managers that do all of the buying and selling. These come with higher fees in order to pay the manager's fees for overseeing the fund's movements.

Indexed-Stocks ETFs

These funds provide investors the option to sell short, buy on margin, and acquire as little as one single share. If you choose to invest in Indexed-Stock ETFs, be watchful of those that might be heavily concentrated on one single industry or a limited number of stocks.

Dividends: Most ETFs pay dividends in proportion to their investment. As a result, you can expect to receive periodic payments for the earnings from the different securities for as long as you hold the fund. If for some reason, the fund is liquidated, you will receive your portion of its residual value.

Taxes

You'll also get to save, as these instruments are more tax-efficient that mutual funds. Because all trading happens through an exchange, there is no need to physically redeem the shares every time a transaction is completed. Since redeeming shares can trigger tax liabilities, conducting all transactions on the exchange keeps you from getting hit with taxes every time a transaction occurs.

Market Impact

Because of the increasing popularity of ETFs, more funds are now being created. This may not be good news for some investors since it means lower trading volumes for many of them. As more funds enter the market, it may become more difficult to buy and sell at such low volumes, which could leave you trapped in an instrument with no way out.

If you choose to invest in ETFs, make sure you select one that can help you to achieve your goals. You should feel confident that the fund you choose will give you the kind of exposure you need to grow your profits. Make sure that you're making your decision based on what works for you and not what others expect.

Start Making Money Now with Peer-to-Peer Lending

Another way to grow your wealth and gain financial freedom is with peer-to-peer lending. In the past, the only way to get a loan for a major purchase was through a financial institution. Now, you can become your own lending institution and collect interest on the money you loan to others. The majority of peer-to-peer loans are used for personal reasons like consolidating debt or home improvements.

How it works

Making a loan with peer-to-peer lending is very different from how they are made with financial institutions. With a traditional loan, the bank will finance the loan with funds deposited from other customers. In contrast, peer-to-peer lending involves matching borrowers and investors through an online lending platform. As an investor, you decide which loans you want to issue and are free to reject those that don't interest you.

There are several lending platforms you can work with. Some have restrictions on the types of people that they allow to make loans, but there are some like the LendingClub.com and Prosper.com that are open to anyone who wants to participate as long as they meet the minimum deposit requirements.

Revenue is generated by charging interest and fees to the borrowers. Some fees including origination fees, late payment fees, and others can come to as much as 6% of the loan. The fee and interest charges vary depending on the platform you use, but be prepared to see some of that money evaporate when payments come in. The lending platform will take a percentage off of every payment made for themselves before sending the balance on to you.

Why peer-to-peer lending?

For the investor, you will receive a higher yield on your money than if you left it in a savings account. It is an easy alternative to investing than stocks and bonds. You don't need a lot of knowledge to get started. You are literally free to diversify your portfolio in any direction you want. And then there is the psychological advantage of knowing that you are doing something to contribute to the advancement of society in many different ways.

Disadvantages

Unlike with financial institutions, your money is not protected by the FDIC. So, if a borrower defaults on a loan, the chances of getting your investment back is slim to none. Also, you won't be able to cash in on your investment if you need the money back before the loan matures. The average term for a loan ranges between three to five years, leaving you without access to your funds for at least that amount of time.

Because this is such a new investment instrument, there is no track record or history to refer to. New trends are being set every day, so there's no way of telling whether or not the industry will continue to be stable.

It is possible to achieve huge returns (sometimes in the double-digits) with this type of lending, but don't allow those figures to distract you from reality. It is a risky investment tool, and you should always proceed with caution.

The 10 Best Strategies for Trading Cryptocurrencies

You've most likely been living under a rock if you haven't heard of cryptocurrencies yet. This new investment tool is believed by many to be the most promising means of garnering massive amounts of money extremely fast. Today, there are probably close to 2,000 altcoins to choose from, and the number is still growing.

Bitcoin, the first and by far the most profitable of cryptocurrencies has pushed itself into the world's consciousness with a whopping rise in price that escalated from a value worth pennies when it was first released to its highest point of nearly $20,000 in December of 2017. But with so many options to choose from, a new investor could easily be overwhelmed.

While cryptocurrencies are probably the riskiest of all investment tools, it doesn't have to be that complicated. If you are brave enough to risk the highly volatile price movements and you think your heart can take the undulations of the waves, here are seven strategies that can help you get into this potentially lucrative market.

ICOs

ICOs or Initial Public Offerings can be very unpredictable because like the stock market's IPOs, these are new coins that are just getting started. When you purchase an ICO, you are literally getting in at the very beginning of a new coin. This means you're going to get the coin at a much lower price than it will be when it is released to the public. This automatically puts you in line for greater profits, sometimes as much as 2500% of your initial investment. However, because it is an entirely new coin, there is also a high risk that it will fail and take all of your money with it. Because there is no insurance protection for cryptocurrency investors, you need to do a lot of research to make sure that the team behind the coin are experienced enough to bring their new baby to life.

- Start by reviewing the list of new ICOs at https://icoranker.com/ and review the ones that interest you.

- Look for the purpose of the coin to determine its supply and demand. Coins that are designed for a limited population may not do well, but coins that have a potential to be useful for a large population can do much better.

- Once you've narrowed your list down to several viable choices, study the team members. You want to know their history, their background, their experience, and whether they can work together to meet the demands of the mission.

- Try to investigate a little further to find out what type of people are already investing in the coin. If they have a good community of investors who are optimistic about their future prospects, then you know they will support the coin and stick with it during the lean times. You can find this information by visiting the various forums set up for each coin.

- What is the legal framework between the development team and other contributors. You should find this information on the coin's whitepaper. The coin's terms and conditions should be laid out in a clear and easy to understand format.

- Visit the website and set-up an escrow wallet. You will be issued a private key you can use to sell your ICOs later.

If you decide to invest in ICOs, don't limit yourself to just one. It is easy for them to fail, so invest in several to increase your chances of success.

The best strategy for ICOs is the buy and hold strategy. The price will fluctuate wildly so don't go into a panic. Hold your coins until you see at least a 50% return on your investment before selling.

Low Price Accumulation

After a coin passes its ICO stage, it gets to join the big boys on the global marketplace. Just like with stocks, you want to buy the coins when the price is low and wait for it to go up in price. Most people will go into a panic when the price takes a significant drop, but seasoned cryptocurrency investors understand that extreme volatility is a characteristic of this type of investment.

Breakouts

By taking advantage of breakouts, you can cut down on your risks, but you need to recognize when these breakouts indicate the start of a new trend. The key to this strategy is to find the best time to enter the market by identifying areas of resistance or support that could be broken under the right conditions. In these scenarios, the coin could break through resistance upward or it can break through support and push downward.

Dollar Cost Averaging

Dollar cost averaging makes it possible for you to invest a pre-set amount of funds on a regular basis on each coin you want to buy. As a result, rather than finding the lowest or the highest price is no longer important. In essence, you are averaging out the overall cost of your coins with each payment. If done over a period of months, the prices generally come out much more favorably than if you were to make a single large payment.

Balanced

One key element in any type of investing is diversification. To successfully diversify, you need to balance your portfolio. This means investing in several different cryptos at the same time. When one coin goes into a slump you can still be earning profits on other coins.

Unbalanced

With an unbalanced strategy, investors designate a set percentage of their funds to coins based on their gut feeling about how well they expect it to perform in the future. Coins that are expected to do well are given the highest percentages while those that are not expected to perform as well will receive a lower percentage.

Profits Earned Reinvested in Other Coins

Once you've made a little money off of some cryptocurrencies, you can begin to diversify your portfolio even further by siphoning off some of your profits and investing them in new coins. By taking 50% of your earnings off of one coin and investing it in more successful coins, you can compound your success.

7 Must-Have Apps for Modern-Day Investors

Getting started in any type of investing can be tricky; even moreso for the new investor. One way to make things easier is to have a little help as you navigate all the potential pitfalls you'll face as you learn.

In the past, this kind of help was once only available to the privileged. Now, anyone can have the information available to capitalize on their growth. With the right apps to guide you, anyone can make decisions like a professional trader. Below are seven of the most effective apps all investors need to have at their disposal.

Stash

The Stash mobile app is the go-to app for investors who are looking to access the best tools for the financial market. It makes it possible for you to purchase low-cost ETFs and stocks directly from your mobile device.

The cost is only $1/month, but for that low price, you get your own investment account and are allowed to make unlimited trades, free education, and the ability to make fractional purchases of more expensive stocks with payments as low as $5.

Vault

The Vault app focuses on older investors ready for retirement. It makes it possible for them to start an individual retirement account (IRA), Roth IRA, or a SEP IRA for those who are self-employed. Investors can direct a pre-set portion of their income automatically towards the plan they choose. So, even if you don't have a retirement plan with your company, you can start investing for a low monthly fee of $1.

Personal Capital

This app gives you regular updates and keeps track of all of the investments in your portfolio. It gives you a regular evaluation of how your investments are performing and suggestions on risk management. It is even possible to quickly check for which stocks are doing the best in your portfolio and which ones you need to make adjustments to. Personal Capital also gives you a comparison of how your portfolio performance measures up against the major market indices.

Stockpile

Stockpile allows you to invest in the stock market in smaller increments. You can buy fractional shares from hundreds of different stocks for as little as $5. There is a small commission fee of $0.99/trade, which is nominal when compared to other services that can charge as much as $10.00.

Parents or other adults can start their children off with a gift card for as little as $20. The small amount pays off in the long run as it starts the young ones off on the right foot learning money management early on.

Wealthfront

This app makes it easy to set aside cash for a college education. Users get a detailed look at their financial situation and can make investments designed to help them to appreciate their capital. You can start small and build as you go. Advice will be given based on the amount of risk you want to take and your financial goals.

E-Trade

E-Trade may seem a bit more expensive than some of the other apps, but with good reason. The app is designed so that researching and trading stocks is about as easy as it gets. You can trade stocks, ETFs, and mutual funds and get all your necessary data in real time. You can even get help in the best ways to build up your portfolio from one of their real live investment specialists.

Robinhood

The Robinhood app opens the doors to new investors by allowing them to make small trades, all commission-free. This is the perfect app if you are still a little hesitant about getting into investing. You can buy stocks, options, ETFs, and cryptocurrencies all zero fees. Their new feature, Robinhood Gold, allows you to trade after-hours and gives you a line of credit so you can make larger purchases if you qualify. There isn't much in terms of trading, research, or personal support, but the platform is simple enough to use and who can beat a no-fee service.

The world of financial investments is changing. We live in a fast-moving digital age, and with more apps like these becoming available, it is now easier than ever for new investors to step on the stage and trade just like a pro.

Conclusion

No doubt, you have discovered a lot of information here that will stir up dreams and ideas for change. Together, we've learned how to break those financial chains so you can literally find your chance at freedom.

Think about it. It doesn't matter where you start, it only matters where you finish. Even if you're so deep in debt that you can't see your way out, it is possible to navigate that maze and find your way to freedom.

It all starts with changing your mind. When you can break those mental chains that may keep you in a "safety zone" then you are free to explore profitable opportunities around every corner. Actions, positive or negative, are the result of how we view our world. If you want to change your circumstances, start by changing your mind.

After identifying the right mindset, we learned how to change your present circumstances so you can get on a better financial footing. We discovered that budgeting can be exciting and enjoyable. Instead of being just an obligation, it becomes a tool for gaining control over your money.

From there, we moved on to how to better manage your credit. After all, if you're going to be growing wealth, good credit will be an essential part of it. This is the magic recipe that could change your life and guide you in the right direction.

But, we also discussed how being financially free meant more than just getting out of debt. We can choose to continue to work for our money or we could find ways to get our money to work for us. Knowing how to invest in stocks, bonds, real estate, or other lucrative opportunities can move us to take risks that we may never have thought about before.

Imagine how your life can change if you didn't have to work for every penny you made. Instead, money just enters your life effortlessly. How awesome would that be? Your health would be better, your mental state would improve, you'd anxiety will be replaced with joy and excitement. You'd be free to spend time with your family, take vacations together, or finally turn dreams into reality.

Whether you choose to invest in the stock market or cryptocurrency, whether you want to try your hand at bonds or real estate, you now have the keys to do whatever it is that you have always wanted to do. It'll take discipline and drive, but gaining that freedom can be one of the most liberating things in your life.

You now have a map to get you to your ultimate goal of financial freedom. Use this book as your guide and refer to it often, but don't just stop there. No matter how exciting and interesting you find the advice in these pages, there is only one way they will work to benefit you, and that's to put them into practice.
Some people can get overwhelmed with this much information and try to put off taking the first step until they understand better. That could delay your chances at success indefinitely. You don't need to know every detail about the stock market to start investing. You don't need to have all the fine points down to buy real estate. All you need is the heart and the desire to make it happen.

So, go ahead — stick your toe in the water and get started. It doesn't matter if you start small, as long as you take that first step. You have the keys to your own financial freedom here. Go back through these pages, create your plan, and get going. You're already halfway there; all that's left for you to do is go for it. There is no time like the present to change your life!

www.ingramcontent.com/pod-product-compliance
Lightning Source LLC
Chambersburg PA
CBHW031126080526
44587CB00011B/1133